The Sail of Cardiff Bay

VOLUME ONE

The Sail of Cardiff Bay

VOLUME ONE

ALAN ROY THORNE

Morgan Publishing
Cardiff

Published in Wales by Morgan Publishing

PO Box 733
Cardiff
CF14 2YX

www.morgan-publishing.co.uk
First Impression - March 2002

ISBN
1 903532 043

British Library Cataloguing-in-Publication Data.
A CIP catalogue for this book is available from the British Library.

DEDICATION

'To 'M' with thanks'.

PORT
of
CARDIFF,
SOUTH WALES.
1855.

CONTENTS

ACKNOWLEDGEMENTS

A book of this type is not really possible without the help and generosity of many people, so many people have helped me that I cannot name them all, but I am especially indebted to the following. My very good friend the late Captain M. Hooper (Graig Shipping) who suggested the book and set me on the right course.

Photographs and assistance have come from numerous sources; T.K. Anderson, Ulster Folk Museum, Tom Bartlett, Berrynabor, Peter Bennett and Dr. David Jenkins of what is left of the once prestigious Welsh Industrial and Maritime Museum at Cardiff Docks, D. Costello Abergavenny, J. Evans Yeovil, Dr. Basil Greenhill and Mrs Ann Greenhill, Captain Murray Henderson, ex 'Pamir', Rick Hogben, the late A.A. Hurst, the redoubtable Bryn Jones and his staff at Cardiff's Central Museum, Harvey Kendall Bude Museum, J. Kennedy Havant, M. Kelly and Andy King Bristol Museum, Trevor Morgan Seascale, Julian Myerscough Penarth, W.H. (Ben) and Mrs Ann Norman Watchet, Anita Pensor and the staff at the Alands Sjofartsmuseum, Rachael Roberts Waterways Trust, Peter Rundle Penarth, M. Sampson National Maritime Museum, Ken Shapley, Estate Surveyor Associated British Ports, Cardiff, Professor Holger Theslett, ex 'Passat'.

Further thanks to Tom Rees for putting together the original manuscript on disc and Sian and Hannah de Claire for editing the final script.

I am grateful to all those mentioned above who gave me permission to use their photographs, especially the owners of copyright material and to all the other people who have helped me in my quest for suitable illustrations. The remainder of the illustrations are from numerous old photographs in my possession acquired over many, many years, sources unknown or forgotten, my inability to remember or trace their original sources precludes any detailed acknowledgement. Finally my thanks to my good friend G. Farquhar and my long suffering wife Muriel.

INTRODUCTION

This book is an attempt to show and record the various sailing vessels, some famous, some infamous that visited Cardiff and Penarth docks especially since the advent of the camera.

Cardiff Bay cannot be found on any old map, chart, or in any old records, the appellation is a recent invention by the P.R. men of the Cardiff Bay Development Corporation, bestowed upon an area known certainly from the sixteenth century as Penarth Harbour. However the name Cardiff Bay serves as a convenient umbrella cover for Cardiff and Penarth docks both of which will be referred to as the Bay ports.

Penarth Harbour c.1820 (Now Cardiff Bay). Water colour by Horner. Llandough left background, Cardiff right background (Courtesy of W.I.M.M)

In the beginning

The earliest water borne visitors to Cardiff Bay could have been a Neolithic person, from West Wales and Southern England, in their crude hollowed logs. Around about 1800 BC the Beaker Folk moved dressed stones from Pembrokeshire to Stonehenge and would have used the safe area of Cardiff bay to dodge inclement weather or await tide changes. Dressed stones from this period have recently been found in the Milford Haven and off Steep Holm.

Iron Age peoples settled along the South Wales coast and established forts at Caerau, Ely, at Cardiff and possibly Llandough. These settlements would have been served by water borne traffic. Sir Cyril Fox and H.A. Hyde expressed the opinion that during the Bronze and Iron Ages there was maritime trade with Ireland and the continent, Cardiff Bay would have been a port of call for traders in the Second Millennium BC.

By 100 BC the Venenti, from Vannes in Brittany, were trading into South Wales and would have used the safe anchorage afforded by the mud flats sheltered from the prevailing westerly winds by the Penarth Head and ridge.

By AD 48 the Romans had reached Gloucester and their vessels, pulled by galley slaves and rigged with a single sail, patrolled the River Severn, known to them as Sabrina, and the Severn Sea. Eventually the Romans established maritime bases along the South Wales coast, including Caerleon, Cardiff, Barry, Colhuw and Neath. Cardiff, by AD 250, had become a major Roman maritime centre, a base for troops of the Second Augustan Legion and a squadron of the Classis Navalis.

The next maritime visitors, unwelcome ones, were Irish raiders in their sinister black hulled, single sail, curraghs. From about AD700 until the Norman period the Vikings in their longboats raided and traded in the Bristol Channel and bequeathed numerous local place names in and around Cardiff Bay, e.g. Cogan, Flat Holm, Steep Holm etc. On at least two occasions they sailed right into the Bay and up the River Taff to sack Llandaff in AD 894 and 915.

Other water borne visitors to Cardiff bay were the ubiquitous Celtic Saints on their peregrinations, sailing to and fro between Brittany, South West England, Ireland, Scotland and South Wales. Saint Dochdwy sailed from Glastonbury and landed on the beach beneath Penarth Head, on the next tide he sailed up the River Ely to Llandough Pill and settled on the high ground behind, establishing a hermitage then a monastery and a little later a school. Saint Barruc, alias Finbarr the patron saint of Cork, a disciple of Saint Cadoc of Llancarfan was drowned when he left his Lenten retreat on Flat Holm and his boat foundered off Barry Island. Saint Decuman sailed to Watchet from South Wales.

Other Celtic missionaries who visited Flat and Steep Holm and would have used Cardiff Bay include saints Athan, Donat, Illtud, Woolos etc. The rock formation that lies between Lavernock point and the Flat Holm, the Wolves, were known in the eighteenth and nineteenth centuries as the Woolies, a possible corruption of Woolos, just up channel off the Flat Holm is another rock formation, the Monkstone.

Legend has it that Robert Fitzhamon, Earl Gloucester, accompanied by 12 knights, 24 squires, 3,000 men plus horses and camp followers sailed from Sea Mills, Avon, and landed at Porthkerry or Penarth. Given the tidal patterns it is most probable that the Normans landed at Penarth.

Between the thirteenth century and the eighteenth Cardiff bay was notorious for harbouring smugglers and pirates. The earliest reference appears to be one of 1233, "Several ships of Kerdif, Newport and Bristol were equipped in the manner of galleys to respectively attack each other". Elizabethan state papers reported, "Cardiff before Penhearthe rode was a familiar and favourite spot for smugglers and pirates". Susan Campbell-Jones records "in the 1500s Cardiff was so notorious as a haunt of pirates that Cardiff merchants abroad dared not admit that they hailed from there".

In 1444 a Welsh pirate, John Davey, left the River Ely, the "Ely ooze" and captured a heavily laden merchant vessel at the entrance to Minehead Harbour, under the noses of the local merchants. Perhaps the most notorious pirate was John Callice who was based at Penarth and brought in numerous prizes, in *1576* he captured a large Spanish vessel, 'Our Lady of the Conception', in the Strait of Belle Isle off the Canadian coast and sailed it across the Atlantic to Penarth. Other pirates who used the Bay ports included 'Brother Battes' Simon Ferdinando and William Chick who was officially described as, "a great doer and chief champion amongst the pirates". Chick with his associate Captain Court regularly used Sully Island as a base. In 1584 Sir John Chichester wrote to Sir Edward Stradling of St. Donat's, the Glamorgan Piracy Commissioner that one of his vessels sailing from Ilfracombe to Biscay had been taken off Land's End by "a red bearded English pirate named Storey", and that Storey in his seventy ton vessel and with his prize were anchored at "Ellye oose nare Cardyffe"

Smugglers' vessels regularly used the Bay ports. A father and son, Richard and Pascoe Robinson from Guernsey established themselves on the Flat Holm c 1730s. Richard had an eighty ton vessel and Pasco a 40 tonner painted bright red with a mermaid figurehead, and ran goods, mainly brandy, tobacco and tea from Guernsey to the Flat Holm then local men ferried the smuggled goods into Cardiff and Penarth. Another notorious smuggler was Edward Edwards, who built a large house on the strand below Penarth Head *c.*1730s; the house became the Penarth Head Inn.

The Bay ports were widely used in fact and fiction. Malory's 'Morte D'Arthur' was written *c.*1469 and was published in 1485 by Caxton. Malory wrote "Lancelot and 100 knights shypped at Cardyf" with King Arthur and Sir Gwaine in pursuit. Earlier it is recorded that in 1319 Leuky Bren, wife of the Senghenydd patriot Llywelyn Bren was brought to Cardiff from Bristol, by sea. And in 1327 Hubert le Despenser put into Cardiff fleeing from his enemies. In 1450 two Sergeants (Valetti) rode on horseback from Tewkesbury to Bristol then sailed to Portishead and then Uphill, they later sailed to the Llandough Pill, to collect rents for the Abbot of Tewkesbury who held the parishes of Liandough, Cogan with their farms and fisheries: "Lord Abbott of Teukesbury collected tithes of the fishery of the Taff as far as Penarth" and "the salmon wear leased to John Morgan Gamag, Gentleman of Llanedern and Roger Morgan of Llandough".

With the ever-increasing number of vessels using the upper Bristol Channel both Penarth Roads and the mud of the Bay assumed even greater importance. The Cardiff Directory of 1796 stated: "3 miles below the town of Cardiff is the harbour called Penarth, and is very commodious for ships and vessels detained in the Bristol Channel by westerly winds". In 1800 the noted antiquarian B.H. Malkin travelled around South Wales and wrote that: "Pennarth Harbour was formed by the junction of three considerable rivers, Taff, Ely and Remny, just where they fall into the sea", and described the harbour as the best and safest harbour in the Bristol Channel except Milford Haven. Alderman Trounce recounted: "I have known vessels lying there wind bound for between two or three months in the winter with strong westerly or south-westerly gales", and later noted: "a fine American clipper the Charlotte A. Stanley laying in Penarth

Roads for 24 days" and that another American vessel the 'African' "had a mutiny by the crew whilst laying in Penarth Roads, several were injured and one James Harley died of injuries ... in the Cardiff Infirmary". G. Farr stated: "Since early times the shipping of the upper channel have anchored in the lee of Penarth Head to gain shelter ... it has been stated authoritatively that on occasions the coastguard counted as many as 500 vessels anchored at one time". This account may have been based on a report in the Cardiff Times, *1865:* "Mr Bryan of Penarth Coastguard Station (he was Chief Coastguard) deposed that from his observatory, 250 feet high, he had taken observations, extending over a period of two months, from 31.12.64 until February 28th 1865... During January he counted 2,284 vessels on the mud-flats in February 2,035 counted".

Ketches and trows River Ely *c.*1900 (Author's Collection)

The opening of the Glamorgan Canal in February 1794 and its extension into the bay in June 1798, and the consequent dock building of the nineteenth century saw a huge upsurge in shipping coming to the Bay ports. This was added to by the large number of sailing vessels built in the Bay. From C 1790 until the 1870s, men such as Joseph Davies, Tredwen, Gunn, Tonkin and the Brothers John and James Batchelor built sloops, smacks, schooners, brigantines, barques and full rigged ships for Cardiff owners and others in Aberystwyth, Cardigan, Leith, Liverpool etc. In the 1850s Hambly and Fifoot had a boat building yard on an extensive spit that ran north, towards Cardiff, from Penarth Head. Here they built barges for local estuarial work and pilot cutters. The yard closed with the building of Penarth Dock *1859-1865*. The dock gates occupy the site of the former boat yard. Hambly and Fifoot moved to Cardiff, in about 1880 Hambly launched a Bristol Channel pilot cutter, the Marianne, which is being restored at Gweek, Cornwall and could be the oldest surviving sailing vessel built in the Bay.

The Bay ports were to be visited by thousands of sailing vessels from the small fry, sloops, smacks, cutters etc, up to the largest barques and fill rigged ships, they also played host to many famous men, the legendary Captain Gustaf Erikson who owned the largest twentieth century fleet of square rigged vessels, Joseph Conrad, and Samuel Plimsoll. Conrad mentions Plimsoll in The Nigger of the Narcissus, the crew are yarning in the fo'c'sle and one of Conrad's characters 'Dirty Knowles'

Bute West Dock *c*.1860's A Forest of Masts (Courtesy W.I.M.M)

holds forth: "I mind I once seed in Cardiff the crew of an overloaded ship'- leastways she weren't overloaded, only a fatherly old gentleman with a white beard and an umbrella came along the quay and talked to the crew ... that 'ere Plimsoll man ... there wasn't one overloaded ship in Penarth Dock at all". Other famous visitors included I.K. Brunel, Tom Mann and Captain Tupper who led the Seaman's National Strike of 1911 from Penarth.

Penarth Dock *c*.1910. Only one sailing vessel centre background

Penarth Dock and the Bute West and East Docks are closed, the Ely Tidal Harbour is to become a 'sport's village' but fortunately the camera captured the great days of sail and serves to maintain the memories of sail of the Bay.

SAIL IN CAMERA

ARCHIBALD RUSSELL

This magnificent 4 mast steel barque was built by Scott of Greenock and launched in 1905 (for Captain Hardie of the Clutha Shipping Company.) The vessel was 291.4 x 43.2 x 24.1 and was the last big square rigger launched from a British yard for the general cargo trade, being able to load 3,930 tons of dead weight. An interesting innovation was the use of bilge keels to lessen rolling in heavy weather, and thus save a great deal of wear and tear of gear.

Under Captain Lowe the vessel was towed from the Clyde to Port Talbot, leaving on February 28th 1905 she arrived on March the 2nd, the tow having taken 42 hours. Loaded with coal the vessel sailed on March 21st and went around Cape Horn to Iquique, Chile, in 103 days.

Just before the start of the First World War the vessel loaded coal at Cardiff and ran out to Rio de Janeiro in 45 days. During the 1920s, the vessel made two visits to Cardiff. On July 25th, 1921, the Archibald Russell left Melbourne loaded with grain and arrived at Queenstown, Ireland, for orders after a slow passage of 115 days, then came to Cardiff to discharge. The vessel was then towed to Milford Haven and laid up.

In February 1924, the vessel was bought by Captain Gustaf Erikson for £7,500 and fitted-out in April by McSymons of Liverpool and Appleby of London. Captain Isidor Eriksson arrived with a crew of young Aland Islanders and completely re-rigged the vessel using 52 coils of manilla, numerous' coils of wire, barrels of oil and cans of paint. Captain Erlkson put the vessel into the Australian grain trade.

On March 4th, 1929, the vessel left Melbourne under Captain K.G. Sjogren and arrived at Cardiff via Queenstown for orders, on June 5th winning that year's 'Grain Race' with a voyage of 93 days, beating many well known passage makers including the Herzogin Cecilie, Lawhill, Ponape etc. In all 14 vessels loaded in Australia and averaged 116.9 days on passage.

On April 3rd, 1939, the vessel under Captain P. Sommarlund left Port Germein, South Australia and arrived at Hull, via Falmouth for orders, on August 2nd a slow passage of 121 days. Twelve sailing vessels loaded and averaged 124 ½ days on passage to Britain. The Archibald Russell was still unloading when the Second World War started, after discharging the vessel was rigged down and laid up at Goole, later being moved to Dunstan on the Tyne where mooring was cheaper. (In 1940 Captain Erikson was still advertising for a crew for the Archibald Russell along with other vessels of his, the Killoran, Lawhill and Pamir).

After the cessation of hostilities the vessel was handed back to Erikson in April, 1947 he had the vessel partially re-rigged and put her up for sale at £5,100 but then decided to trade with her between the Mediterranean and the River Plate but with Captain Gustaf Erikson's death in August 1947 the idea was dropped. The Archibald Russell was eventually scrapped at Gateshead in 1949.

"Archibald Russell" idling on a calm day. The gunports painted on the hull suggest the vessel was still under Hardie's house flag. (Rick Hogben collection)

"Archibald Russell" (P. Rundle collelction)

A.G. ROPES

The "A.G. Ropes" was one of the greatest square-rigged vessels built in New England, USA, between 1870-1 880s, when a large fleet of strongly built, fast and economic cargo carriers were built at ports on the American eastern sea-board. The vessels were known from their ports of origin as 'Down-Easters'. Basil Lubbock described the vessel as. "A splendid ship and a famous, beautiful Down-Easter" and "the finest full rigger under the Stars and Stripes". The vessel of 2,401 tons with dimensions 258.2 x 44.7 x 28.3 was built of wood at Bath, Maine in 1884 for Captain I.F. Chapman. The Master of the vessel from 1884 until it was sold in 1906, was Captain David H. Rivers, a son-in-law and business partner of I.F. Chapman. Rivers was described as being, "amongst the most noted sail carriers", and under his skilful guidance the vessel maintained a wonderful average in her passages, out and home, around Cape Horn. The vessel also kept singularly free from trouble.

In 1906 the vessel described by Basil Greenhill as "a magnificent American wooden full-rigged ship" was handed over by Captain Rivers who had sailed the vessel with great success to every part of the world, to the Luckenbach Transportation and Wrecking Company of New York to be used as a barge.

In early 1906 the "A.G. Ropes" discharged her cargo at Bristol and was towed to Penarth to load coal for Hong Kong.

"A.G. Ropes" waiting to load coal for Hong Kong, Penarth Dock 1906
(Courtesy N.M.M)

BROOKLANDS (SUSAN VITTERY)

The "Brooklands" was built in 1859 by Kelly at Sandquay, Dartmouth for Vittery and Company of Brixham and launched as the "Susan Vittery", a two mast top-sail schooner of 140 tons with dimensions 100.6 x 21.4 x 12.1, and spent her early years in the Azores orange trade. The vessel is credited with making two voyages in six weeks between London and St. Michael's, Azores. The vessel was then put into the Newfoundland codfish trade, making voyages to Crete, Greece, Portugal and Spain. Douglas Bennet who served on her in her later years remembered her as being a fast vessel but "must have been a regular submarine on the Newfoundland run".

In 1879 Mr Vittery sold the vessel to a Mr Hawkey of Brixham who, in turn, sold her to Newquay owners in 1884. A third mast was added in 1903, which was easier on the men and gear. In 1918 the schooner was acquired by Mr Parker of Grimsby and practically rebuilt at Whitstable. In 1923 Parker sold the vessel to Captain

Creenan of Ballinacuna, County Cork, who renamed her "Brooklands", and traded between Ireland and the Mersey and Bristol Channel ports. Basil Greenhill saw the vessel in this trade in the 1930s, "I remember her one summer's evening ... crawling across the narrow neck of the Severn estuary between the Breaksea and Selworthy, outward bound from Cardiff to the west of Ireland." Michael Bouquet relates on seeing the "Brooklands", "in 1941 in driving rain between the Helwick and Scarweather lightships in the Bristol Channel, slogging to the westward under a press of sail bound for Cork with a cargo of Welsh coal". Even in old age the schooner could press on, Bouquet relates, "in a powerful motor vessel it took us nearly the whole watch to catch and pass her".

"Brooklands" at Gloucester Docks in excellent order
(courtesy Waterways Trust) F.H. Lloyd.

The "Brooklands" was the last engineless schooner trading around Britain and traded right throughout the Second World War, with Captain Creenan, his son, as mate, and a crew of four with an additional hand signed on for long voyages. In 1944 all the Irish coasting schooners were mobilised by the Irish government and put under joint management to aid the country in the acute coal shortage, some 12 schooners, including the "Brooklands", carried over 40,000 tons of coal across the Irish Sea, mainly from South Wales ports, including the Bay ports.

With the profits made during the war an engine was installed in 1946, and in 1948 a complete set of new sails was acquired. Around 1950 the vessel was re-fitted with the intention of trading between Liverpool and the West Indies. This however came to naught and the vessel was lost in 1953 near the Tuskar Rock. The vessel's longevity says much for the skill of her builders. Just before the loss of the vessel she was again named "Susan Vittery".

CAMBORNE

A three mast square topsail schooner launched at Amlwch in 1884 by W.C. Paynter & Co. for Thomas Morgan & Co. of Amlwch, "a schooner of graceful shape and good qualities", the gross tonnage was 118 on dimensions of 93.2 x 22.5 x 10.1. The vessel was bought in 1918 by W.A. Jenkins of Swansea who later sold it to the Hook Colliery of Haverfordwest, in 1920, to carry Hook coal to various French ports and the colliery company installed an engine to facilitate faster and more reliable passages.

"Brooklands" under reduced sail coming in to anchor (Author's collection)

In 1922 the "Camborne" was bought by the redoubtable Captain Shaw of Gloucester, who used her in the Irish trade wherein the vessel made regular good passages, e.g. Bridgwater to Shannon 48 hours, Sharpness to Queenstown 26 hours. Whilst in Limerick, in 1922, the vessel came under sustained gunfire; fighting between the Government troops of the Irish Free State and the Irish Republican Army was taking place, with the opposing troops on opposite banks of the River Shannon and with the "Camborne" moored in between. Captain Shaw remembered, ... I believe the "Camborne" got more than a fair share of the bullets. We had them in the hull, mast, rigging, and this shooting went on for days". On a later visit to Limerick the vessel was taken over by the Free State Army to transport supplies and soldiers to Cork, countermanding orders were received and the "Camborne" was used to ferry 300 troops to a steamer anchored lower down the river.

The "Camborne" carried salt from Gloucester to Ireland, coal to Cornish ports, one unusual voyage was to carry cider apples from Connah's Quay to Cherbourg, her main trade however was salt or coal to Ireland with timber or pit props back and as such was a common sight in the Bay either to load, unload or to shelter. In February 1936 loaded with salt from Gloucester for Tralee the vessel was put onto the safe mud of the Bay to dodge "one of the fiercest easterly gales anyone could remember". In 1991 Captain H.K. Shaw recalled the bad weather of early 1936. The "Camborne" loaded salt at Gloucester for Fenit, Southern Ireland, the vessel with Captain Hugh Shaw in command and his son Humphrey Kenneth as mate, plus two crewmen, left Sharpness and arrived at Penarth Roads with the weather deteriorating.

At this time, 1936, Penarth Dock was officially closed to commercial traffic although the lock gate men were still working to allow vessels access to the Pontoon dry dock for repair, and to lay up in the dock. Shipping agents for the small coastal sailing craft had made arrangements with the dock owner, the G.W.R. to allow the ketches and schooners to shelter in the Dock Basins for just a few shillings, so much easier than anchoring on the mud-flats of Cardiff Bay. The "Camborne" entered the basin, the schooner "Earl Cairns" was already berthed there. The "Earl Cairns" was built by Ferguson and Baird of Connah's Quay (see Kathleen and May) in 1884, a wooden 3 mast top sail schooner of 127 tons; she was hulked at Falmouth in 1945. After a couple of days the "Camborne" left Penarth and sailed down channel, the weather again worsened, blowing hard from the south-east, and put into Milford Haven and anchored in Angle Bay, among the large number of sailing coasters already sheltering in the bay were the schooners "Earl Cairns", "Kathleen and May" and the Slade's "Margaret Hobley."

Captain P.J. Walsh, MNI, AMIPR, remembered that in 1941, aged 16, he joined the steamship "Lakewood", loading coal at Cardiff's East Dock, in the West Dock were two vessels he had served on, the schooner "Camborne" and the ketch "Irene", both unloading timber from Ireland.

The "Camborne" traded right through the Second World War and in 1946

Captain Hugh Shaw sold her and retired. He had been at sea under sail for 50 years, 42 of which he had been the Master of various sailing vessels. The "Camborne" was sold to Maltese owners who re-named her the "Carmary".

"Camborne" entering Cardiff *c.* 1936.
In background two steam ships at the Windsor Quay (W.I.M.M.)

"Camborne" bowling along with squaresail set flying (B. Greenhill collection)

C.F.H.

A ketch built at Calstock, just north of Plymouth in 1892 by James Goss, her dimensions were 74.0 x 20.4 x 9.3 with a net registered tonnage of 56 tons and gross tons 76. The first owner was Will Hamley of Plymouth, who named the vessel after his son Charles Francis Hamley. In 1911 the vessel was acquired by the French owners and re-named "Yolande" and she ran between the West Dock, Cardiff and various French ports, coal out and timber, especially pit props on the return voyage. In 1914 she was bought by H.G.Clarke of Braunton and re-registered as "C.F.H." Clarke installed an auxiliary motor in1915, but her rig was never reduced during the time she ran as an auxiliary. During the First World War she served as a fleet tender at Scapa Flow and during the Second World War served as a supply vessel to the Royal Navy, in 1935-1945. Between the wars she worked all around the coasts of Britain.

The "C.F.H." was possibly the last vessel to unload onto a beach, in the upper

reaches of the Bristol Channel, at Knightstone Weston-super-Mare. G. Farr recalled, "In 1933 I saw the ketch "C.F.H." unloading her coal into motor lorries which drove down the slipway".

At the end of hostilities in 1945 the vessel was laid up at Appledore then, with a reduced rig she became a motor vessel with sails as secondary propulsion, really nothing more than "steadying sails", and as such traded in the upper Bristol Channel, Ely Tidal Harbour, Lydney, the Buffer Wharf Chepstow etc. in the 1950s the vessel became a houseboat at Upton-on-Severn, where her remains now lie.

"C.F.H." at Weston-Super-Mare *c.*1930's unloading Ely Harbour coal. (W.I.M.M.)

"C.F.H." at Chepstow in the 1950's alongside the Gloucester Trow "Victory" (W.I.M.M.)

CHARLOTTE

Built at Southampton in 1864 by C. Langley, 73-ton net reg., gross tonnage 140, rigged as a ketch. The vessel was owned at Watchet from 1892 until 1927, previously she was owned by Butler of Braunton.

In May 1901 the "Charlotte" was owned by Captain Thomas Davis of Watchet, with Captain Searle, Master, and the vessel traded between Ireland and various Bristol Channel ports. Later the vessel was owned by the Wansborough Paper Co. of Watchet, with Captain Frank Norman as Master. In April 1916 a blizzard of great fury and suddenness drove the "Charlotte" ashore at Blue Anchor near Watchet. Captain Norman and his crew had to fight their way through waist-deep snow to reach Watchet. The ketch was re-floated and was used to carry coal, mainly from the Penarth, Ely Tidal Harbour to Watchet. In 1927 the vessel was perhaps the last, engineless vessel to enter the Ely Harbour, towed up by the tug, ironically named the 'Norman". In 1927 the vessel was broken up at Watchet and its timbers used to construct a large shed now used by the Watchet Boat Owners Association.

"Charlotte" from a painting by M.J. Norman (W.H. [Ben] Norman collection)

"Charlotte" being broken up in Watchet harbour 1927.
The building to the left is the infamous London Inn (W.H. [Ben] Norman collection)

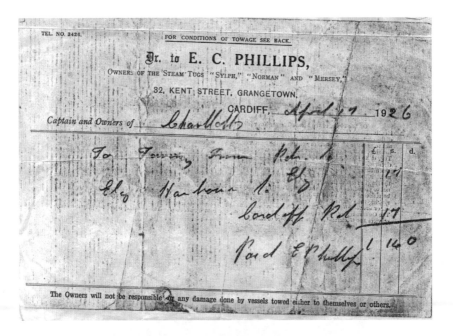

£1-14-0, the price of towing the "Charlotte" in and out of the Ely harbour 1926
(W.H. [Ben] Norman collection)

CHARLOTTE RHODES

One of the most famous schooners of the twentieth century, the "Charlotte Rhodes" became a household name due to her 'starring role' in the popular BBC series 'The Onedin Line'. The vessel was built as the Danish trading schooner "Meta Jan", 95 tons, in 1904 and traded as such in the Baltic and North Sea. In October 1964 the "Meta Jan" of Skive and the "Traly" of Tuborg Havn both ran aground off Langesund, in Southern Norway, while bound for the fertiliser plant at Heroya on the Skienfjord. Both were re-floated without any damage.

The "Meta Jan" was acquired by English owners and brought to Dartmouth, where she was re-rigged as a traditional 3 mast square top-sail schooner, and as such was regularly seen in the Bristol Channel and paid a courtesy visit to Cardiff in June 1977. The vessel was lost some years later, being completely gutted by fire at Amsterdam in 1977.

"Charlotte Rhodes" moored at Barrow, Cumbria (T. Morgan collection)

"Charlotte Rhodes" River Thames, London (R. Hogben collection)

CRAIG'S COUNTIES

The Bay ports were at their busiest that is in regard to the number of vessels using the ports as opposed to total tonnage loaded, in the period 1860-1900. During this period the Craig Line vessels, all named after a county but which should not be confused with the Welsh County Line of W. Thomas and Co., regularly used Cardiff and Penarth. The Craig fleet contained 21 iron ships, most of them 4 masters, and one iron barque, the vessels were built between 1863-1887, the first 10 were built by Connell of Glasgow, the others by Barclay, Curle and Company.

The "County of Aberdeen" was built in 1879 by Barclay Curle, an iron 4 mast ship of 1,865 tons on dimensions of 281 x 40.4 x 24.1 with a good turn of speed. In 1880 sailing from Bombay to Calcutta in 15 days. Loaded with Welsh coal the vessel left Cardiff on December 21st 1884 bound for Bombay and was never heard of again.

On December 21st 1884, the "County of Caithness", a 4 mast ship of 1,646 tons, 266.4 x 38.8 x 23.6, built by Barclay, Curle left Cardiff and arrived in Bombay after a passage of 117 days. On April 18th 1887, again loaded with coal, the vessel left Cardiff and reached Calcutta after 97 days. In 1903 the vessel was sold to the Norwegians who re-named her "Sofie" and re-rigged her as a barque.

In 1878 the 1,640 ton "County of Dumfries" was built by Barclay, Curle, with dimensions of 266.2 x 38.8 x 23.6. Loaded with coal she left Penarth in 1893 and arrived at Mauritius after 66 days. In 1905 the vessel was sold to the Russians and renamed "Sovinto". The same builders launched the "County of Edinburgh" in 1885, an iron 4 mast ship of 2,078 tons, 285.6 x 42.5 x 24.3. Captain F.W.J Tode took her straight from the launching, and the vessel's maiden voyage was from Cardiff with coal for Bombay, arriving after 92 days. On September 16th 1899, she left Penarth and arrived in Cape Town after a passage of 51 days. Two years later the vessel left Cardiff on June 7th and arrived in Cape Town on July 17th 50 days out. In 1903 the vessel was sold to the Germans who re-named her "Frieda" and re-rigged her as a barque, later the vessel was bought by Mr Lundquist of Marichamp.

"County of Edinburgh" (R. Hogben collection)

"County of Dumfries" (R. Hogben collection)

The "County of Peebles" was launched in 1875 by Barclay, Curle, an iron 4 mast ship of 1,614 tons with dimensions of 266.6 x 38.7 x 23.4. The vessel made at least five voyages from Cardiff.

1880 Cardiff to Bombay, an 83 day passage
1881 Cardiff to Aden, an 84 day passage
1884 Cardiff to Bombay, a 94 day passage
1885 Cardiff to Bombay, an103 day passage
1886 Cardiff to Bombay, a 99 day passage

In 1892 the vessel went from Penarth to Mauritius in 66 days, the vessel was sold in 1898 to the Chileans.

The "County of Lancaster", built by Connell, left Cardiff for Bombay in 1885 and1886 and made passages of 95 days and 91 days respectively. The "County of Roxburgh", built by Barclay, left Cardiff 1887 for Calcutta and again in 1891 sailed to Colombo, both passages took 85 days. Other "Counties" included "Ayr", "Bute", "Selkirk" etc.

The "County of Peebles" ended her days as part of a breakwater at Punta Arenas, Straits of Magellan, and the "County of Roxburgh" ran aground in 1905 onto an atoll (Takoroa) in the South Pacific, and her remains can still be seen.

CUTTY SARK

This vessel must qualify as one of the most famous sailing vessels and fortunately can still be seen at Greenwich, London. The "Cutty Sark", a genuine "Tall Ship", square-rigged on all masts and crossing a main skysail above the royals, was built by Scott and Linton of Dumbarton to a design by one of the partners Hercules Linton for Captain John Willis. The vessel was 921 reg. Tons, 212.5 x 36 x 21 and launched on November 22nd 1869 for the China tea trade, and made her maiden voyage from London to China, leaving London February 1870 for Shanghai. The "Cutty Sark" made eight voyages in the China tea trade, but the Suez Canal, opened November 1869, ended the hegemony of the clippers running in the tea trade as steam vessels increasingly used the canal.

Willis put the vessel into general cargo work, whilst in New York, March 1880, 9 ft 6 inches was taken off the lower masts, 7 foot off the lower yards and the upper masts and yards were shortened in proportion, which meant the vessel lost her sky sail yard.

The "Cutty Sark" left London in Ballast on May 6th 1880 and arrived at Penarth on May 22nd to load coal for the American Navy Department's Pacific Fleet at Yokohama. On the vessel's arrival at Penarth most of the crew left the vessel largely due to the vessel's 'bucko mate', a "hard fisted, despotic character" Sidney Smith. Captain Wallace found difficulty in getting a crew, his task not made any easier by the mate's sinister reputation. Eventually five Englishmen, three Danes, three Negroes, two Greeks and one Italian were signed on.

Captain Wallace sailed from Penarth on Friday June 4th and the foc's'le's 'lawyer' immediately began to prophesy the well-known consequences. The "Cutty Sark" had barely left Penarth before she had to return and anchor in Penarth Roads whilst a strong Southwest gale tore up the Bristol Channel for three days. The vessel left on June 7th and dropped the pilot off Lundy Island.

The mate, Sidney Smith, continually vented his spleen upon the three Negroes, especially one, John Francis. They argued continually and eventually fought, whilst Captain Wallace, pistol in hand, threatened to shoot anyone who tried to interfere.

When approaching the Sunda Straits, the mate gave Francis an order, which was ignored; again Smith called out to Francis and again the order was ignored. Smith rushed Francis who was armed with a capstan bar; the men grappled, Smith gained the bar and smashed it on the Negroes head. He was knocked unconscious and never regained consciousness, dying three days later.

The crew became mutinous, the mate stayed in his cabin, with Captain Wallace taking his watch. Whilst anchored at Anjer awaiting orders, the Captain smuggled the mate onto an American vessel, the "Colorada". The crew on finding out refused to work, so Captain Wallace raised anchor and set sail with just the apprentices and petty officers. For days the vessel drifted towards Yokohama, then when four days out from Anjer the Captain walked to the stern of the vessel and stepped on to the taff rail and jumped overboard. The crew launched a boat but a long search proved useless, a number of sharks were seen swimming furiously in the area!

"Cutty Sark" (R. Hobgen collection)

"Cutty Sark at Greenwich" (R. Hobgen collection)

Two years later, under the alias of Anderson, Sidney Smith was recognised in London, taken into custody, tried and convicted of manslaughter and sentenced to seven years hard labour. He eventually ended up as skipper for the Anglo-American Oil Co. and died in February 1922, aged 73.

The story became "a well-known yarn in ship's foc's'les for many years" and Joseph Conrad put it into one of his books. He wrote to his friend A.T. Saunders of Adelaide on June 14th 1917, that the "Cutty Sark" incident had inspired the 'Secret Sharer...''was suggested to me by a young fellow who was second mate on the "Cutty Sark". The story was well remembered in the Merchant Service even in my time". Conrad could have heard the story whilst serving as second mate on the "Narcissus" or as second mate on the "Tilkhurst", both vessels having loaded coal at Penarth, or whilst staying in Penarth and Cardiff while the "Tilkhurst" was loading at Penarth.

Between 1882 and 1895 the vessel made 12 voyages between Britain and Australia, in the wool trade, averaging 4,750 bales of Australian wool on return. In July 1895, the vessel was sold to Ferreira and Co. of Lisbon for £2,100 and in 1905 she was in Cardiff loading coal for Portugal. Later in 1919 she was in Swansea. In 1922 the vessel was bought by Captain Dowman and returned to England.

DENBIGH CASTLE

A 3 mast ship of 3078 tons built in 1884 by W.Hamilton Port Glasgow owned by R. Thomas of Liverpool left Cardiff on October 9th, 1908, loaded with a cargo of patent fuel for Mollendo, a small port in Peru, which meant a passage around Cape Horn known to old 'shell-backs' as Cape Stiff.

Staten Island, off Cape Horn, was sighted on December 11th with the weather deteriorating and for the next three weeks the vessel battered against very strong contrary winds, during which the cargo shifted and the vessel developed a serious list. Finally the Master, Captain Evans, abandoned the rounding of the Horn and turned east, the crew then spent seven dreadful days in total darkness trimming the cargo. Captain Evans set course for Fremantle, Australia, where the vessel arrived 253 days after leaving Cardiff {having been eight and a half months continually at sea. At anchor off Fremantle the crew became mutinous and eventually the ringleaders were arrested by the Australian police and jailed.

The Denbigh Castle left Fremantle, after taking on supplies, and four months later the Andes were sighted. Three days later, the vessel anchored at Mollendo and Captain Evans was replaced by Captain Higgins. Whilst the vessel was being discharged at Mollendo, and then later loaded with guano at the Lobos de Terra islands, nine hundred miles north of Mollendo, the crew again grew mutinous. Captain Higgins called the mates, apprentices, cook and carpenter aft and devised a plan to entice the ringleaders aft, cosh them then tie and gag them. This plan worked and a full-blooded mutiny was averted.

The vessel eventually sailed and reached the River Scheldt two years after leaving Cardiff. A year later the "Denbigh Castle" sank on passage from Lobos D'Afuera to Antwerp, wreckage from the vessel was washed ashore at Bridport.

DE WADDEN

Originally a very smart and trim 3 mast, steel built, fore and aft auxiliary schooner of 239 tons, built by Gebr Van Diepon at Waterhuizen, Holland and launched in 1917. Her overall dimensions are 116.8 x 24.4 x 10.3 and rather unusually the vessel had water ballast tanks. In 1922 she was bought from Amsterdam owners by Hall's of Arklow, and run in the Irish Sea trade. During the Second World War she made a number of voyages to Portugal. John McCaffrey remembered, "the late captain R.T. Hall of Arklow conveyed many cargoes of barley in the "De Wadden", loading at Wexford for the Guinness brewery at Dublin.

"De Wadden" *c.*1940's loading pit props at an unknown Irish river
(B. Greenhill collection)

After the cessation of hostilities in 1945 the vessel was confined to sailing between the Mersey and Bristol Channel to Irish ports, Arklow, Wicklow, Youghal etc., coal to Ireland and timber or pit props as a return cargo. As one of the last trading schooners her movements were closely chronicled in the Sea Breezes (April, 1958) "The "De Wadden" continues in the Irish Sea ... Garston at the end of January loading for Youghal and Arklow ... has since made a trip to Waterford", (March, 1959) ... "docked at Garston on January 5Th and sailed 12 days later with coal for Youghal", (October, 1959) ... "De Wadden still in the Irish Sea shuttle services", (October, 1960)... "De Wadden on the Irish trade, also an occasional run over to Cardiff to load coal for County Cork ports."

Captain Robert Price, Arklow, was the vessel's Captain when the vessel was sold to Scottish owners who worked her, carrying ballast on the Clyde, the vessel would run ashore at the Kyles of Bute and 230 tons of sand would be loaded and sold in Dunoon.

This work ceased in 1977 and the vessel was laid up until being bought in 1984 by the Merseyside Maritime Museum who restored the vessel, which now lies at the Albert Dock, Liverpool.

EILIAN

A steel-built three mast topsail schooner built at Amlwch in 1908 by William Thomas and Son with dimensions of 102.6 x 21.9 x 9.4 and a gross tonnage of 140. The vessel was built for the general coasting and near continent trades, especially Welsh slates to Antwerp and Hamburg. In 1928 the vessel was bought by S. INCLEDON of Braunton and until 1939 was mainly in the Cornish china clay trade. During the Second World War, and then until 1957, the "Eilian" pottered about between the Bristol Channel ports with occasional runs over to Ireland. The vessel was a frequent visitor to the Bay ports. Noel LLF. Tringham wrote in the "Sea Breezes", "The "Eilian" was on a regular gas coal run, Cardiff to Ilfracombe."

In 1957 the vessel was sold to Danish owners who used her in Danish waters until selling her to trade in the West Indies under the ownership of Earl Byron Clarke, she was still trading as a motor vessel in the 1980s.

"Eilian" loading coal for Ilfracombe at the Ely tidal harbour,
August 1954 alongside tip number 3 (T. Morgan collection)

"Eilian" off Penarth Dock entrance. Cardiff Docks in background and the
"Emily Barrett" at anchor. Fresh easterly blowing as the
"Eilian" leaves the Ely bound for Ilfracombe (T. Morgan collection)

"Eilian" off Combe Martin North Devon, 1954 (T. Morgan collection)

"Eilian" alongside at Ilfracombe 1954, ready to discharge
(T. Morgan collection)

"Eilian" unloaded Ilfracombe 1954 (T. Morgan collection)

ELGINSHIRE

A 4 mast steel barque built by Birrell, Stenhouse of Dumbarton for Messrs. Law and Co. for their Shire Line. The vessel of 2,160 gross registered tonnage, dimensions 285 x 40.5 x 24.7 was launched in May 1889. The vessel's first captain was Robert Greig, followed by Captains Hannah, Stoll, Wright and Dixon, in 1919 Captain David Roberts, who had been born in Dolgellau in 1870, took command, he had gone to sea aged 14 on the schooner "Mary and Ellen of Aberdovey".

The "Elginshire" left Melbourne, September 9th 1921 with grain for the UK, she met a good deal of foul weather on her run to Cape Horn and after rounding the Horn was badly battered in the North Atlantic. After calling at Queenstown for orders she arrived at Cardiff, a passage of 144 days out of Melbourne. On arrival at Cardiff the vessel ran aground and had to be lightened by unloading some of her cargo into barges before she was re-floated. 144 days was a slow passage, 68 vessels sailed from South Australia that year with grain for the UK. The average passage was 131.4 days. The fastest passage was made by the "Marlborough Hill", Port Lincoln to Cardiff 91 days, the second fastest was the "Kilmeny", Melbourne to London 98 days.

After unloading the vessel was towed to Milford Haven and laid up, Captain Roberts lived aboard for 3 months then left to command the "Garthgarry", the owners then sold the "Elginshire" to the ship breakers.

"Elginshire" (R. Hobgen collection)

"Emily Priscilla" Roath Dock, Cardiff May 1928 alongside S.S. Steadfast discharging grain (W.I.M.M.)

EMILY PRISCILLA

The "Emily Priscilla" was one of the last Severn trows to be built, in 1894, and was still trading up until the Second World War. She was built at Chepstow for T. Haling of Deerhurst with a Net Registered Tonnage of 67.

EMMA LOUISE

W. Westacott the noted boat builder of Barnstable built his last wooden vessel in 1883, a topsail schooner the "Emma Louise" for S. Berry of Barnstaple with dimensions of 75.4 x 19.8 x 8.3 and Net Registered Tonnage 66. In 1926 the vessel was re-rigged as a ketch and an engine was installed.

Captain P.S. Rawle of Minehead bought the vessel in 1928 and traded within the Bristol Channel and to Ireland. The ketch was usually running coal from Lydney or the Ely Tidal Harbour to Minehead and was the last trading vessel owned in that small Somerset port and was always beautifully kept: "clean deck, varnished masts and brightly painted". Captain Rawle was also Harbour Master at Minehead and could remember when there were coal freights of three shillings a ton from the Ely to Minehead, when a crewman's wage was £2 a trip, for which he had to help trim the cargo in the loading port and assist in its discharge at Minehead.

"Emma Louise" at Minehead c. 1950 loaded with coal for the gasworks, now demolished.
(W.H. [Ben] Norman collection)

"Emma Louise" under reduced rig, on her last commercial voyage 1953
(W.H. [Ben] Norman collection)

The "Emma Louise" carried her last cargo in 1953 and was then laid up in the River Torridge where she slowly broke up. Her hulk can be seen on the riverbank, halfway between Appledore and Bideford, along with two other ketches and a schooner.

FALLS OF EARN

The famous Glasgow Falls Line had nine Russell built 4 masters; the company was formed by Wright and Breakenbridge in 1878.

The finest and fastest was also the largest, the lovely "Falls of Earn", with two sky sails, a beautiful "Tall Ship". Their first vessel was the "Falls of Clyde launched in 1879 and now preserved at Honolulu. The "Falls of Earn was launched by Russell on May 30th 1884, 2,292 gross tons with dimensions 302.6 x 42.1 x 24.5.

On April 10th 1891 the vessel left Penarth loaded with coal for Acheen in Sumatra, she arrived off Acheen Head on 1st July, 1891 dropped anchor at midnight but unfortunately she sat on her anchor and sank in shallow water, her deck was only 4 foot underwater. Salvage attempts were not successful and she was abandoned and the wreck auctioned for $500.

"Falls of Earn" (R. Hogben collection)

FAVELL

The last of a great fleet of square-riggers built by C. Hill and Sons of Bristol, the Favell somewhat unusually was built under a shed and launched in 1895, a trim three mast barque with a white hull, 237.5 x 36.2 x 21.3, and of 1,363 tons gross. The vessel was named after C. Hill's daughter, who later became Lady Milnes, and was taken from the stocks by Captain Young. After a couple of years the vessel was sold to

"Favell" (R. Hogben collection)

J.W. Soderlund of Raumo and then ten years later to Gunnar Dydman of Helsingfors, and for decades the vessel was in the Australian grain trade.

On April 16th 1934, the Favell left Port German, South Australia and made a slow passage, via Cape Horn, to Cardiff arriving on September 11th a passage of 148 days. During 1934 22 vessels loaded Australian grain and sailed to Britain, the average passage being 123 days, the fastest passage was the "Magdalene Vinnen", 91 days from Port Victoria to Dublin.

After discharging her grain in Cardiff the vessel sailed in ballast to the Baltic and was broken up at Viborg.

FLORA (POTOSI)

This massive vessel 4,026 tons gross with dimensions of 366.3 x 49.7 x 28.5 was built by Teckenborg at Geestmonde and launched in 1895 for the famous firm of Hamburg ship owners Laeisz and became one of the most famous of the 'Flying P. Line'. (All Laeiszes vessels carried the capital 'P'.) The "Potosi" was one of only 7 square rigged vessels built with five masts, a five mast barque setting a massive sail area of 55,000 square feet to drive a hull designed to carry 6,000 tons of Chilean nitrate. Even given the size of the vessel she was "very swift and handy".

The "Potosi" was skippered on her maiden voyage and for some years after by the most famous and successful square rig skipper Captain Robert Hildendorf, who took her out to Chile on her first passage in an astonishing 66 days. In 1900 under Hildendorf the "Potosi" sailed 378 nautical miles in 24 hours, an average of just under 16 knots, and once ran for 11 days at an average of 11.2 knots.

Hildendorf in 20 years with the 'P' line commanded 9 'windjammers' and rounded Cape Horn 66 times and consistently made two round trips in less than 12 months, Hamburg to the ports of North West Chile. His average passage was 64 days out and 74 on return.

At the outbreak of the First World War the "Potosi" was in a Chilean port and was seized and allocated to the Italians who immediately sold her to Gonzales,

"Flora", ex-"Potosi" (R. Hogben collection)

Soffin and Company of Valpariso who re-named her "Flora". The "Flora" left Cardiff in September 1925 with coal and coke for Mejillones, in the South Atlantic, the cargo caught fire, two explosions occurred and brought down one of the masts, the vessel was abandoned and sank by gunfire from an Argentinian cruiser.

The other five-masters were the "France" (1890), "Maria Rickmers" (1890), "Preussen" (1902), "R.C. Rickmers" (1906), "France II" (1912) and the "Kobenhavn" (1921). All the five-masters were barques with the exception of the "Preussen"; a five-mast fully rigged ship.

GARLANDSTONE

A ketch of 75.75 gross tons, with dimensions 76.0 x 20.2 x 9.0 built on speculation by James Goss at his yard at Calstock, and was launched in 1909 after being bought whilst laying on the slip way by Captain John James Russan of Studdulph, Milford Haven. The vessel could carry 100 tons of cargo and traded between Bristol Channel ports and ports on the south and west coasts of Ireland.

"Garlandstone" off Instow, River Torridge 1946, naval vessels laid-up in background
(B. Greenhill collection)

In 1912 an engine, a twin cylinder paraffin engine built by Brazil Straker and Co. Ltd., Bristol, was installed, but Captain Russan did not reduce her sail area. In 1919 the vessel was bought by Captain A.Murdoch of Gloucester who sailed the vessel until 1941. The late Edmund Eglinton who sailed in the "Garlandstore" in the 1920s remembered Captain Murdock as, "a big and tall man (who) ... wore a bowler hat at sea and ashore ... he explained the bowler saying he was always knocking his head against deck beams ... and the bowler was protection.

In 1941 having discharged in an Irish port, the Irish crew refused to sail back to the Bristol Channel. Captain Murdock, by then about seventy, set sail with the aid of a few hobblers and sailed alone to King Road, off Portishead, where he anchored having spent 48 hours on the passage. The crew of a local tug helped him stow the sails and towed the vessel to Lydney, where he ended his life at sea and sold the "Garlandstore" to Charles Couchman of Gloucester, who ten months later sold the vessel to L.A.Wingfield of London. The vessel continued in the Irish trade commanded by a Polish aristocrat Micha Leszcynski with fellow Poles as crewmen. In August 1943 the Parkhouse family of Braunton bought the vessel with John Newcome also of Braunton as a major shareholder.

"Garlandstone" laid-up Bute West Dock, Cardiff 1960 (T. Morgan collection)

In 1944 a modern engine was installed and the vessel's sail area was reduced and she traded inside the Bristol Channel until 1958, visiting Lydney, the Ely Tidal Harbour etc. The vessel was acquired by an American who held the ownership for three years when the vessel was acquired by Messrs Kyffin and Lansdown of Porthmadoc. The Garlandstone has been fully restored and now lies on the Tamar at Morwellham Quay.

GRACE HARWAR

A three mast full rigged ship launched in 1889 by Hamilton for W. Montgomery of London, an extremely handsome vessel of 1,877 tons gross with dimensions of 266.7 x 39.1 x *23.5*. In February 1912 the vessel arrived in Cardiff having been towed from Hamburg to load coal for South America.

In 1913 the vessel was sold to Rederi A/B Delfin of Helsingfors who sold her to Gustaf Erikson in 1916, although remembered as a 'regular' in the Australian grain trade especially the 'The Grain Races' between 1922 and 1932 she also took timber from the Baltic to Australia, saltpetre to Bristol, timber from Canada to Australia, coal from Swansea to South Africa, guano from Peru to North Carolina, fertiliser from England to Mauritius and only four grain cargoes from South Australia to Britain.

The "Grace Harwar" loaded grain at Port Augusta, South Australia and left on February 3rd 1927, called at Queenstown for orders and arrived in Cardiff in June, a passage of 136 days. Seventeen vessels were in the 'Grain Race' that year and the average passage was 131.9 days, the fastest passage was made by the "Herzogin Cecilie", 98 days Port Lincoln to Hamburg. After discharging her grain at Spiller's the "Grace Harwar" was towed to Swansea to load coal for Luderitz Bay, South Africa. Erikson sold the vessel to the breakers in 1935.

"Grace Harwar" (R. Hogben collection)

GREAT BRITAIN

One of the most famous sailing vessels to enter the 'Bay' was I.K. Brunel's "Great Britain". She was floated from her building dock into Bristol's Floating Harbour on July 19th 1843. She was an iron-hulled vessel of 3,270 tons, a screw driven six-mast schooner, the first ocean-going screw driven vessel and the world's first six-mast schooner.

The vessel's maiden voyage was from Liverpool, July 26th *1845* to New York followed by three more transatlantic passages, at the start of a fifth crossing the Great Britain ran aground on the Irish coast. Re-floated, the vessel languished for three years in Liverpool. Back at sea, the vessel served as a troop ship in the Crimean War and the Indian Mutiny. Her most successful period was between 1852-1876 on the Australian passenger and cargo run, and as a troopship.

"Great Britain" just after launching at Bristol 1843 (B. Greenhill collection)

In 1882 the vessel's engines were removed and she was re-rigged as a three mast pure sailing vessel, as such the "Great Britain" made a number of voyages to San Francisco, coal out, grain back. In early 1886 the vessel docked at Penarth to load coal for South America, and left Penarth on February 6th under Captain Henry Stap. Trying to make her westing around cape Horn she ran into hurricane force winds, the cargo shifted, leaks appeared and the fore and mizzen topgallant masts came down. Battered by continual gales the crew had to work in the black hold, trying to re-trim the cargo with shifting boards. Eventually the captain brought the vessel about and ran to the Falkland Islands, promptly running aground on William Isle, re-floated the vessel again ran aground and was then towed to Port Stanley by the steamer "Rance".

She was brought back to the UK in 1970 and is now berthed in the dock where she was built. During her long career the vessel, originally a six master was reduced to a five master in 1846 then a four master in 1852. In 1856 the Great Britain was further reduced to a three mast steam vessel and in 1882 with her engines removed she became a three mast fully rigged ship.

"Great Britain" leaving Penarth 6th February 1886.
The vessel is shown in ballast rather than loaded
(Courtesy 'Hi-Plan' Office Services, Penarth, copywright Owen Eardsley)

HALDON

A large ketch built by the Hawke Brothers between July 1892 and March 1893, at their Stonehouse Yard, Devonport, the vessel was 96 tons net registration with dimensions 88 x 21.6 x 9.9. Originally the vessel was owned in Topsham then Southend. In 1902 the vessel was bought by Orkney islanders and traded between the islands and the Scottish mainland until 1916, when the vessel was bought by the Hook Colliery Co. of Haverfordwest. In 1922 the Colliery Co. had a fifty brake horsepower Invincible installed and later that year sold the vessel to the Slade family for £1,200.

During the 1920s with Captain W.J. Slade as skipper/owner, the vessel ran salt from Gloucester, in the company of the "Camborne", to the bacon factories of south-west Ireland, and coal from Lydney and the Ely Tidal Harbour including a regular contract to run coal from the Ely to Padstow for a three month period in the autumn. If given good weather, the "Haldon" could do two trips a week, "but given sometimes a fortnight on one". The "Haldon" was heavy on her gear, so in 1924 Captain Slade converted the vessel to a three mast, fore and aft, schooner.

Captain Slade kept the "Haldon" in the Irish trade until the first years of the Second World War. In 1940 the "Haldon" and five other vessels, the schooners "Kathleen and May", "Margaret Hobley" and "M.A. Jones" both owned by the Slade family, and the ketches "Bessie Ellen" and "Progress" also owned by the Slades left Penarth Dock, with a south-east wind, bound for Irish ports, the "Haldon" was loaded with coal for Waterford.

One of the last voyages of the "Haldon" with Captain Slade in command, a short one, was a cargo of barley from Bristol to Swansea in 1943. The vessel left Bristol and got to Penarth mud, "where I was wind bound for several days". In 1944 Captain Slade sold the vessel for *£2,500,* then in 1948 she was sold to continental owners and the vessel was still trading in Icelandic waters in 1955.

"Haldon" off Instow River, Torridge (B. Greenhill collection)

HERZOGIN CECILIE

This beautiful barque was built in 1902 by Rickmers at Bremerhaven and named after the Herzogin (Duchess) Cecilie von Mecklenburg-Schwerin. The steel four-mast barque had a gross tonnage of 3,242 with dimensions 310.0 x 46 x 24.8. She was built as a working school ship for the Norddeutscher Lloyd Company and fitted out to the highest standards, not only a cadet ship and large cargo carrier, but as a floating "showpiece for the Germany of the Second Empire.

The vessel's maiden voyage was from Bremerhaven, June 27th 1902 to Astoria via Montevideo for repairs. The 'Duchess' left Astoria with grain on February 20th 1903 calling at Falmouth for orders and arrived in Cardiff on June 10th. On February 28th 1908 the vessel left Adelaide and arrived off Queenstown for orders, May 31st 1908, arriving at Cardiff on June 4th. After discharging her grain cargoes, in 1903 and 1908, the vessel returned to Bremen in ballast.

In 1921 Captain Gustaf Erikson bought the "Duchess" for £4,500 and put his senior skipper, Captain Reuben de Cloux in command, and he was to command her during her most successful years, 1921 - 1924 and 1925-1929, mainly in the Australian grain trade.

On January 19th 1928, the vessel left Port Lincoln with grain and anchored off Falmouth for orders on April 24th, reaching Cardiff on April 27th. After unloading, the vessel sailed in ballast to Mariehamn, Erikson's base.

Under Captain Sven Eriksson the "Herzogin Cecilie" left Port Lincoln on January 28th, 1936, and reached Falmouth on April 23rd for orders. The vessel left Falmouth on April 24th and at 3.45 am April 25th went ashore at Soar Mill Cove, Bolt Head, Devon. Re-floated and taken in tow the vessel was taken to Starhole Cove on June 19th a salvage was attempted but to universal disappointment the vessels back

"Herzogin Cecilie" Bute East Dock, Cardiff, April 1928,
with Alan Villiers in the crew (W.I.M.M.)

broke on July 17th, and the Master, Eriksson, finally abandoned ship on September 9th. The vessel, a wreck, was sold for scrap on September 24th 1936, the end of Gustaf Erlkson's favourite vessel. Underhill regarded the "Herzogin Cecilie" as "one of the best known and probably the most photographed of all the modern sailers".

"Herzogin Cecilie" ashore South Devon 1936 (R. Hogben collection)

HOBAH

The "Hobah" was built in 1879 on a small beach at Trelew Creek, just off Mylor Creek, Cornwall, by Thomas Gray, a master shipwright of Falmouth. He was the vessel's first owner with his partner Captain Philip Quenault who commanded the vessel, mainly between Britain and the ports of western France. The vessel, in her early years, carried Cornish granite to the Mediterranean for dock building - a hard trade that says much for the shipwright's skill.

The vessel was a Net Registered Tonnage of 56 with dimensions 78.6 x 19.9 x 9.6, and was bought by Lem Hyett and Captain Charles Lamey in 1908. In November 1908 the vessel, loaded with Welsh coal, took from November 29th 1908, until January 29th to get into Bude to unload, after discharging another three weeks were spent, because of continuing bad weather, waiting to get out. The crew paid off, wages for three months were £2.00 the wages for the voyage. In 1911 a 30bhp engine was installed which meant the vessel was less dependent on the weather and Captain Charles Lamey was succeeded by his son, Captain William Lamey the vessel being used between the Welsh ports and those of South West England.

The "Hobah" was the last ketch to unload coal at Newquay, Cornwall in 1922, and in 1937 was the last to discharge on the beach at Port Luney, Cornwall. The vessel's last voyage was in June 1940, the "Hobah" loaded coal at Penarth for

Appledore, not long after leaving Penarth the engine broke down and the vessel took five tides to sail the short passage to Appledore, she never went to sea again and was laid up in the Torridge alongside the "Emma Louise".

"Hobah" in the Torridge *c.*1920, loaded and awaiting discharge at Appledore, photograph by the late H. Oliver Hill. Although motorised, the rig has not been reduced

(B. Greenhill collection)

INVERMORE

This vessel can claim to be the last merchant schooner launched in home waters, a wooden three-mast schooner built in 1921 with an auxiliary engine. The "Invermore" was a husky vessel of Irish oak and larch which sailed well and fast, and was an excellent sea boat. The vessel was of 146 tons gross with dimensions of 92 x 22.4 x 11 and was built by John Tyrell and Sons of Arklow, with John Tyrell as owner/ master.

The "Invermore" traded between Ireland and the Mersey, the South Wales coal ports and the western ports of the English Channel. In 1938 a new, more powerful engine was installed, and on February 4th 1939, Captain Tyrell died on board while the vessel was anchored at Passage East, County Waterford. The vessel traded into the 1950s and in 1959 was sold out of trade, the Sea Breezes, October 1959, reported: "... the Irish schooner "Invermore" was still laying in Dublin ... when her overhaul is

"Invermore" at Whitehaven (T. Morgan collection)

completed a local crew will take her out to Denmark where ... she is now owned".
Later in 1959 the vessel was bought by a group of Englishmen who planned a world
voyage, money ran out and the vessel was laid up off Rough Point in the River Dart,
opposite the Royal Naval College and slowly broke up. Her remains can still be seen
at low water.

"Invermore" leaving Whitehaven (T. Morgan collection)

IRENE

The "Irene" was the last trading vessel built at Bridgwater, launched by J.F. Carver
and Sons in 1907, the vessel's dimensions were 85.5 x 21 x 9.1 with a Net Registered
Tonnage of 77.96 Gross Tonnage, and was initially owned by C.J. Symons, C. Symons
and Captain W. Lee all of Bridgwater. Captain Lee was the vessel's first master and
originally traded to the continent and also in the brick trade to Liverpool and Ireland. In 1919 a 4Ohp Invincible engine was installed, replaced in 1923 by a 7Ohp
Bolinder.

In 1922 the "Irene" was purchased by Captain Shaw (see "Camborne"), and his
wife's second brother, Captain Ira Aldridge became the vessel's master. The "Irene"
was in the Bristol Channel to Ireland trade and also traded around the Irish coast, on
one occasion loading a cargo of live pigs at Dingle for Tralee the pigs being loaded
lose in the hold on top of earth ballast.

Captain Shaw sold the vessel back to the Symons in 1928 and she traded mainly in the Bristol Channel and became a frequent visitor to the Bay ports, in 1939 a 90hp Ellwe Swenska engine was installed, having come out of a Humber ferry, the vessel's Captain was now Captain Schiller who stayed with her until her last trading voyage in 1960. As with the "De Wadden" the "Irene's" last years of trading were well documented, e.g. Basil Underhill wrote, "I thought her as dainty a little craft as one could wish to meet", and in the Sea Breezes, April 1959, "Irene busy between Avonmouth and Pembroke", October 1959, "Irene still on Avonmouth cattle feed trade" and in December 1960, "Irene has been advertised for sale by her owners Colthurst, Symonds ....in recent years she has worked mainly between Avonmouth to Milford, Pembroke and Appledore with cattle food under Captain Schiller".

In 1960 the vessel was laid up at Appledore alongside the last British wooden trading schooner the "Kathleen and May", and in 1961 the "Irene " was sold out of trade and three of the last sailing skippers in Trade, Captains Schiller, Tom Jewell ("Kathleen and May") and Peter Herbert ("Agnes", "Emily Barrett"), sailed the "Irene" around to the Hamble. In 1965 she was bought, and saved, by Dr. Leslie Morrish, who has had the vessel fully restored, put a 135 hp diesel engine in her and now sails the vessel under charter.

"Irene", Cardiff *c.*1936. Although an engine has been installed
the vessel has not had its rig reduced (W.I.M.M.)

"Irene" at anchor, photographed from Penarth Dock (T. Morgan collection)

"Irene" as a charter vessel *c.*1980's (W.H. [Ben] Norman collection)

ISABELLA

A small, very fast two mast fore and aft schooner, built by Gibbs of Yealhampton in 1864, a vessel of 61 tons on dimensions *75.8* x 18.7 x 8.1, the original owners were Captain Tippett of Fowey, who commanded her for many years, and Messrs J.W. Todd and Co. also of Fowey, who traded with her between the Channel Islands and ports in Cornwall and Devon. The famous John Stephens of Fowey bought the "Isabella" in 1893 and lengthened her lines forward into a graceful clipper bow and gave her square yards on the fore mast and placed her in the Atlantic salt-fish trade. Stephens had a large fleet of schooners, at its greatest between 1890-1910, when his oldest schooner was the "Royal Adelaide", built in Cardiff in 1830 and bought by Stephens in 1906.

The North Atlantic trade was very arduous, the "Isabella" however sailed well and must have been an easy vessel to work, usually with a crew of only four and on one occasion, three. The crewing arrangements were most unusual, two Captains and two boys just out of school. The "Isabella" is famous for the following amazing record. She left Fowey in ballast for St. John's, Newfoundland, on May 10th 1899, where she loaded fish for Portugal. She arrived back in England on the 23rd November 1899 having made three trips with Newfoundland fish to Portugal, six passages back and forth across the Atlantic in six months and 18 days.

However, it was not all plain sailing. The winter of 1911/1912 was particularly hard on the small schooners of the North Atlantic trade. The "Isabella" left St. John's for Oporto on November 17th 1911 and put into Cardiff on December 22nd 1911 having been battered all across the Atlantic and sustaining damage to her bulwarks, spars, sails and rigging. On December 18th the log recorded: "10pm made lights at Hartland

"Isabella" lying at Fowey (courtesy Royal Institute of Cornwall. B. Greenhill collection)

(Devon) ... blowing hard from the south-south west" ... "shaped course for Cardiff wind squally". On 19 December the log read: "heavy, squally south-south west winds with heavy rain ... 8am. Wind flew to Northwest. Nash Point abeam ... 11am came to anchor in Cardiff Roads with port anchor and 30 fathom of cable". The vessel docked at Cardiff badly damaged and with the crew exhausted, after discharging the cargo of fish the vessel went around to Fowey for repairs. The "Isabella" was lost on October 12th 1913, hitting rocks at the entrance to St. John's, Newfoundland.

JONADAB

A large sea-going trow, the "Jonadab" (a biblical name) was built at Newport in 1848, Net Registered Tons 68, for J. Miles of Bristol, in her heyday she made numerous voyages to Ireland and the ports of the English Channel. Originally built with an open hold, she was rebuilt with side decks and hatches in 1895 to allow for deep-sea passages. The vessel was a ketch and set a quadrilateral jackyard topsail, much favoured by the ketch rigged trows.

In 1949 when owned by Mrs James of Saul, Gloucester, the "Jonadab" was turned into a motor barge and it says much for the strength of the vessel that being over one hundred years old the hull could take the strain of a heavy diesel engine. As a motor barge the "Jonadab" traded in the Upper Bristol Channel until 1963.

The "Jonadab" was a familiar sight in the Bay both as a ketch and as a motor barge. In 1963 the venerable vessel was hulked at Lydney. The strength of her hull and her seaworthiness was proved in 1983. After lying on the riverbank just down river from Lydney Dock an exceptional spring tide took her on an unsupervised voyage up to Sharpness Dock - the call of the sea was still strong. The vessel

"Jonadab" *c.*1900's fully rigged off Portishead (author's collection).

blocked the dock entrance and was towed by indignant dock officials to be beached across the river just up stream from Lydney where she slowly fell apart.

"Jonadab" being towed down the Avon, Bristol to South Wales to load coal
(Bristol Museum).

"Jonadab" being towed up the Avon loaded with Welsh coal
(Bristol Museum)

J.T. and S.

Launched in November 1918 the "J.T. and S." was a wooden three-mast schooner built with an auxiliary engine, and setting a large spinnaker instead of a square sail. The vessel was built by John Tyrrell and Sons of Arklow with oak and birch all grown within five miles of Arklow; the schooner was of 121 tons with dimensions 95 x 22 x10. In 1938 a new, more powerful engine was installed.

Captain John Tyrell once sailed the vessel from Cardiff Roads to Waterford Harbour in three days, the engine was out of action, John Tyrrell (Jun) was in the crew and recalled the passage, stating, "It was fine summer weather, with nothing but cat's paws all the way, the mate claimed she was sailing by the heat of the sun".

The schooner was employed trading from Ireland to the ports of the Mersey, Upper Bristol Channel and the western ports of the English ports, usually oats or pit props were loaded in Ireland with coal as a return cargo. The Sea Breezes, April 1958, reported that the vessel loaded at Garston for Youghal and Arklow and on September 25th, 1958, the "J.T. and S." carried pit props to Birkenhead and this was

"J.T and S." loading coal at a Cumbrian port (T. Morgan collection)

one of her last commercial voyages. The Sea Breezes, March 1959, reported that the vessel was, "Laid up for disposal". Later in 1959 she was bought by a group of Englishmen who intended using her as a training vessel, but she foundered off Start Point in 1960 and was lost.

KATE

In 1911 Captain H. Shaw (see "Camborne") and his father-in-law, Captain Lewis Aidridge bought the two masted topsail schooner "Kate" of Barrow. During the first years in Shaw's ownership with him as Master, the vessel traded between the Mersey and Bridgwater carried dressed granite from Penryn to Erith, fertiliser to Cardigan and cargoes to Southern Ireland. In November 1914 the "Kate" loaded coal at Newport (Mon) for Youghal, after leaving Newport the vessel stayed a night in Penarth Roads then made a good trip to Youghal. This voyage was the start of a regular trade from Newport and the Bay ports to Youghal, Kinsale etc.

In 1917 the "Kate" delivered pit props, from Ireland, to Newport and loaded coal for Fecamp, as a return cargo Captain Shaw loaded flints at Fecamp for Cardiff. After discharging the flints a cargo of coal was loaded for St. Brieve. This trade between Cardiff and Fecamp, St. Brieuc, Paimpol, Lizardrieux, Morlaix etc. continued until January 1920 when Captain Shaw sailed to Portmadoc to install an engine, and returned to the Irish trade.

"Kate" waiting to load at Bridgewater, vessels loading gear rigged on the main-mast. Note ancient crane behind bowsprit (T. Morgan collection)

During 1922 Captain Shaw purchased the "Irene", and put his brother-in-law Captain Ira Aidridge as Master. Shaw also bought the "Camborne" and took command, putting his brother William as Master of the "Kate". The three vessels then ran in the Irish trade, but by 1928 Shaw was forced to sell both the "Irene" and the "Kate", the "Kate" went for just £450.

KATHLEEN AND MAY

This handsome three-mast schooner was launched in April 1900 as the Lizzie May, built by Ferguson and Baird at their Connah's Quay yard for Captain John Coppack and named after his two daughters Elizabeth and May. The schooner was of 136 tons gross and 99 net, with dimensions 98.4 x 23.2 x 10.1 ft, and carried double topsails on her foremast.

The schooner's maiden voyage was from her home port to Rochester in Kent under the command of a Connah's Quay mariner, Captain Tom Hughes. Her next voyage was to Plymouth with cement, then Cardiff with pitch, where after unloading she loaded coal for Falmouth.

In September 1908 she was sold to M.J. Fleming of Youghal, Ireland, and re-named "Kathleen and May". In October 1908 whilst on passage from London with cement for Newport, Mon. she ran aground on the Goodwin Sands, re-floated, was taken to Dover and unloaded. In ballast she left for Milford Haven, hit by heavy weather off Lundy Island the "Kathleen and May" ran for the shelter of Penarth Roads. Under Captain Joe Aherne of Youghal the vessel now entered the coal trade between the Bristol Channel and her Irish base, oats or pit props out with coal on return from Wales.

"Kathleen and May" in the Torridge in 1961 (B. Greenhill collection)

On April 23rd 1931, the schooner put into Youghal with 202 tons of coal from Cardiff, the last cargo she was to carry under sail alone. Later that year the vessel was bought by Captain Tom Jewell and his father William, two well known Appledore mariners, the vessel was refitted for £800 and a Beadmore 80 bhp engine was installed, her topsails were taken down and her top masts shortened. Until 1939 the vessel sailed in the Welsh coal trade to Youghal and voyages to small west Cork harbours, Courtmacsherry, Castletownend etc.

When the Second World War started the vessel was 'armed' with a Lewis gun and a rifle and continued in the Irish Trade with coal, and china clay from Fremington near Barnstable to Crosshaven in County Cork for the famous pottery at Carrigaline. In July 1943 a new engine a Deutz of 125 hp was installed, then in March 1952 a new £3,000 diesel engine, a four cylinder Crossley of 135 bhp was installed.

Throughout the 1 950s the schooner "Kathleen and May" an anachronism in the rocket age was a common sight off Penarth, the Sea Breezes reported in March 1959: "In the Bristol Channel the "Kathleen and May" has made a few trips between Cardiff and Appledore, but has not been fixed for Eire recently", then in the April issue: "the "Kathleen and May" active . . running between Avonmouth and Pembroke". In early 1960 the "Kathleen and May was in Crosshaven alongside the "De Wadden" after discharging china clay from Fremington.

"Kathleen and Mary", St. Katherine Dock, London (R. Hogben collection)

The schooner made her last commercial voyage in September 1960, Captain Tom Jewell was now 65 and Bristol Channel freights were becoming hard to come by. The vessel's last cargo was coal from South Wales to Par in Cornwall. Laid up at Appledore the vessel was bought in 1961 for £4,000 to become a passenger cruiser, this plan came to naught and the vessel changed hands several times whilst lying at Cowes and then at Littlehampton. In 1966 Captain Paul Davis of Llantwit Major bought the schooner and brought her around to Barry Dock where she lay from July 1966 until June 1967 when she went back to Appledore. For three years she lay in the Torridge then was saved, being bought by the newly formed Maritime Trust. The vessel was fully restored and moored at Sutton Harbour, Plymouth before being moved to St. Katherine Dock, London, eventually being moved across the River Thames to Southwark.

KILLORAN

A particularly attractive steel three-mast barque built by the Ailsa Shipbuilding Company at their Troon yard, launched on June 30th 1900 for Miss Corsar of Arbroath. The barque was *1,523* net, 1,757 gross tonnage with a cargo capacity of 3,100 tons on dimensions of 261.5 x 39.5 x 22.7.

Her maiden voyage started at Arbroath on August 20th 1900, out to Montevideo. For the first twenty years of her cargo carrying, the vessel sailed mainly to South American ports, e.g. Rio de Janeiro, Iquique, Tocopilla, etc., with four passages to Australia.

The "Killoran" left Cardiff on February 12th 1903, with coal for Acapulco and again in March 1919 left Cardiff with coal for Buenos Aires. In May, 1912, the vessel left Swansea with coal for Rio de Janeiro and in September 1913 loaded coal at Barry for Montevideo.

In 1908 the vessel was bought by J. Hardie and Co., of Glasgow, who ran the vessel until November 1921 when she was laid up. Gustaf Erikson bought the Killoran

"Killoran" (R. Hogben collection).

for £2,600 on February 23rd 1924, and captain K.J. Erikson sailed her from Grange-mouth on April 25t 1924, for Antofagasta. Until 1939 the vessel was in the Australian grain trade, the captain from 1933-37 was Captain Verner Bjorkfelt, a sailing master of vast experience and consummate skill who sailed the "Killoran" into Ipswich Docks, without a tug, in August 1936, this saving of a towage fee would have pleased Gustaf Erikson who was known as "pjutte Gustaf', "pjutte" translates as "stingy".

On February 27th 1940, the "Killoran" left Cardiff with coal for Buenos Aires towed by the tug "Bristolian", Captain W.H.V. Bevan, that had taken on bunker coal at the Ely Harbour, Penarth. The tug took the "Killoran" twenty miles west of Lundy before dropping the tow. After discharging at Buenos Aires the vessel left for Las Palmas, at 15.39 hours on August 10th 1940, she was sunk by the German armed merchant cruiser "Widder". Korvetten-Kapitan von Ruckteschell had his crew place time bombs in the bow, stern, and amidships, Captain Leman and the crew of the "Killoran" were taken to France and interned.

LADY ISABELLA

This beautiful steel four mast barque loaded coal in Cardiff C1890, the vessel was owned by the North British Shipping Company, Glasgow, and was lost sometime later wrecked on the Oregon coast.

"Lady Isabella" about to load coal at Cardiff.
Her condition suggests she has just come from dry-docking (Author's collection)

LAWHILL

A steel four mast barque of 2,942 tons gross built by W.B. Thompson of Dundee in 1892 for Captain Barrie of Dundee, the vessel's dimensions were 317.5 x 45 x 25.1. The vessel's first commercial voyage appears to have been from Penarth in 1893 loaded with coal for Colombo, a passage of 90 days. In 1899 the vessel was bought by Anglo America Oil Company and under Captain J.C. Jarvis made some smart passages. In

"Lawhill" (R. Hogben collection)

1911 the vessel was sold to G. Windram and Co. for *£5,500*, three years later she was bought by A. Troberg of Mariehamn for *£8,500*. Then in 1919 Captain Gustaf Erikson added the "Lawhill", which he came to call "my lucky Lawhill", to his fleet.

Erikson ran the "Lawhill" in the South Australian grain trade up until the start of the Second World War. The "Lawhill" arrived at Barry on June 23rd 1935, 124 days out from Wallaroo. The vessel's average passage time from S. Australia to Europe whist under Erikson's ownership was 121 days. The "Lawhill's" best passage in the "Grain Race" was

"Lawhill" fully laden at the end of voyage, being towed into an unknown dock (P. Rundle collection).

106 days in 1931 under Captain J.A. Soderlund, leaving Adelaide on February 11th and arriving at Birkenhead, via Queenstown for orders, on May 28th.

When the Second World War started, the "Lawhill" was discharging Australian grain in Glasgow having made a slow passage from Port Lincoln, the "Lawhill" had left on March 15th and arrived at Glasgow via Falmouth for orders on August 2nd 1939, a voyage of 140 days. On May 3rd 1940, the vessel left Troon for Montevideo in ballast. In the South American port the vessel received orders to proceed to the Assumption Islands and the Seychelles to load guano for Auckand. After discharging at Aukland the "Lawhill" loaded grain at Port Lincoln for East London, South Africa, arriving there on July 23rd 1941. On August 21st the vessel was seized as a 'War Prize' by the South African authorities.

A prize court allowed the Finnish Master, Captain A. Soderlund, to keep command and with a mixed crew, members of his old crew and South African trainees, he traded throughout the war between South Africa and Australia, and proved to be very profitable. The vessel traded until 1946, latterly under captain M. Lindholm.

In 1946 the vessel was put up for auction and was bought by the Portuguese who took her to Laurenco Marques where she lay for some years, and was eventually scrapped.

MARLBOROUGH HILL

In 1884 Potter's launched the "Holt Hill" and in 1885 launched her sister ship, the "Marlborough Hill", a four mast barque crossing three skysails over double topgallants and royals, the iron vessel was of 2,443 tons with dimensions 300.5 x 42.2 x 24.7 and was built for William Price of Liverpool who named all his vessels

"Marlborough Hill ", a rather distressed photograph shewing the vessel moored to a buoy.
The sails have an excellent 'harbour stow', but the washing on the forecastle is
blowing free (Aland Sjofartsmuseum).

"Hill", not to be confused with the "Hills" of J.R. Dickson of Glasgow. The vessel was initially in the South American run, coal out, nitrate or guano back.

By 1914 the vessel had passed to Robert Mattsson of the Aland Islands, who dispensed with the skysails. During the First World War the "Marlborough Hill" was stopped by a German submarine, in a heavy sea the Master and crew of the barque were ordered to abandon ship, in attempting this both the ship's boats were smashed. The Master asked the submarine commander, "... what shall I do", the answer was, I leave you", a lucky escape!

On September 17th 1921, the vessel left Port Lincoln, loaded with grain and arrived in Cardiff via Queenstown, in 91 days the fastest passage that year in the 'Grain Race'. In 1921, 68 vessels left South Australia for Europe, the average passage being 131.1 days. Another eleven sailing vessels arrived at Cardiff from Australia, in 1921 including the "Archibald Russell" 115 days, "Edmund Rostand" 120 days, "Elginshire" 144 days, "Terpsichore" 145 and the "Woodburn" 117 days.

The "Marlborough Hill" left Wallaroo, Spencer's Gulf, South Australia, 1923, and arrived at Cardiff via Queenstown in 151 days, a far cry from her 1921 passage, such are the vagaries of the sea. The vessel left Wallaroo on January 23rd 1923, that year nine vessels loaded grain and the average passage was 133.1 days. The vessel was sold to the Italians who scrapped her.

"Marlborough Hill" under reduced rig in a 'bit of a blow' (W.I.M.M.)

MERIONETH

The "Merioneth" was launched in 1875 by Royden's for Hughes and Company, an iron ship of 1,366 tons with dimensions 231.4 x 38.9 x 23.6; the vessel was soon sold to the Davies Windmill Line. Under the Davies house flag the "Merioneth" arrived at Falmouth for orders on August 23rd 1887, 159 days out from San Francisco, a particularly slow passage. After discharging at Dublin the vessel loaded coal at Cardiff and on October 16th 1887, under the command of Captain Robert Thomas sailed for San Francisco and arrived after a fine passage of 96 days.

The "Merioneth" left San Francisco on April 8th 1888, and anchored off Queenstown for orders, 95 days out and then discharged, again, at Dublin. The little "Merioneth" was still trading in the early 1920s, under the Italian flag, with auxiliary engines. The vessel appears to have been scrapped around 1922.

Most Welsh maritime historians and others of international repute, such as the late Basil Lubbock, credit the "Merioneth's" 1887 voyage from Cardiff to San Francisco as a record, this can be disputed. The Senator made the same voyage in 89/90 days in 1889, which would appear to be the record for an iron ship.

MISTLETOE

This small ketch, Net Reg. Tonnage 45, was built by W. Date at Plymouth in 1890 for T. Ley of Combe Martin. Captain Ley was a member of the renowned Ley family of whose extended family continually crop up in the maritime history of North Devon and Somerset as coasting skippers, harbour masters etc.

"Mistletoe" at Topsham, Devon, 1936. The vessel still has a lofty topmast
and lengthy bowsprit. The loading gaff and gin are in place with a grab at deck level
(B.Greenhill collection).

The "Mistletoe" worked all the Bristol Channel ports, including the smaller ones like Porlock with coal from the Ely Tidal Harbour, and regularly landed coal on the beach at Glenthorne just down channel from Porlock.

Thomas Ley owner and master of the "Mistletoe", typical of the sturdy coasting men (W.H. [Ben] Norman collection)

MONKBARNS

A full rigged ship of 1,971 tons built by A. McMillan and Son of Dumbarton and launched in 1895 for D. Corsar of Liverpool, the 'Flying Horse Line', the vessel's dimensions were 267 x 40.1 x 23.6.

In 1904 the "Monkbarns" ran from San Francisco to Falmouth in 110 days and in 1906 outward bound to San Francisco she was trapped in the ice south of Cape Horn and held for 63 days during the bitter Antarctic weather during which time her master, Captain Robinson died. In April 1911 the vessel was bought by the John Stewart Company for £4,850. The "Monkbarns" sailed from Cardiff on February 5th 1917 with coal for Montevideo then went in ballast to Newport News to load coal for Buenos Aires and then out to Melbourne in ballast.

In 1918 the "Monkbarns" was lying alongside the Railway Pier, Williamstown, Melbourne, loading a cargo of flour to discharge at New York, for the United States Army. A very mixed bunch were signed on to complement the already cosmopolitan crew, the new crewmembers included an Irishman, Welshman, Yank, Dutchman, Peruvian, Dane, Norwegian and a Chilean, a mixed bunch indeed. The vessel left Melbourne on March 20th 1918. The vessel was immediately hit by bad weather which steadily worsened, and within days the crew were complaining about the food. The Irishman led a deputation, armed with knives, onto the poop, eventually many of the crew refused to work. Matters worsened and as the Horn approached, May 15th the mate started carrying a loaded revolver and the next day the Captain issued revolvers to the second and third mates.

On May 19th the mate wrote in his log, "Since leaving Melbourne the crew have been in an obvious state of mutiny, causing the Master and Officers much anxiety and trouble". The Irishman, T. O'Brien, was caught stealing salt meat, on May 30th, and was shot in the leg by the mate. After rounding the Horn the mate logged on June 5th "The crew are in a state of mutiny and insubordination". On June 7th, the Irishman, Welshman and the Dutchman refused to work and were soon followed by the starboard watch.

Captain Donaldson set a course for Rio de Janeiro and sailed in with distress signals flying, the "Monkbarns" sighted HMS "Armadale Castle", a Union Castle passenger liner on war duty, and signalled, "the crew have mutinied and threatened to kill the Captain". Sub-Lieutenant G.M. Frost, RNR, with a sergeant, corporal, lance-corporal and nine men of the Royal Marines, boarded the "Monkbarns" and a number of the crew were arrested including O'Brien, Thomas the Welshman, the Dane Sorensen and the American, Peruvian and Norwegian. The men were tried at a Naval Court on HMS Armadale Castle and all were found guilty and put in the cells, eventually they were taken to the UK and landed at Newport, Monmouthshire.

The "Monkbarn's" next voyage, her sixth under Stewart's flag with Captain Will Davies in command, was from Cardiff loaded with coal for Las Palmas. She left on June 26th 1920, and arrived at Las Palmas 15 days later. The vessel's last voyage was in 1926; she left Valparaiso on January 20th 1926 and had to put into Rio de Janeiro on March 28th where her Master Captain William Davies, of Nevin, Carnarvonshire died at the age of 76. Captain Davies had first gone to sea, aged 14, in the barque "Eifion" followed by two other

"Monkbarns" (R.Hogben collection)

famous Welsh vessels the barques "Gwytheyrn Castle" and "Gwydr Castle". The "Monkbarns" left Rio on April 1st under her Chief Officer Richard Davies and took 99 days to Gravesend. The vessel lay idle in the Thames until February 1927 when she was bought for £2,500 by the Norwegian whaling company Brun and van de Lippe of Tonsberg, who had her towed to Port Talbot to load coal. She left Port Talbot, in tow, on March 4th 1927, and ended up as a coal hulk at Corcubion in Northern Spain.

MOSHULU

The "Moshulu" a very large 4-mast barque launched by Hamilton's of Port Glasgow in 1904 for G J H Siemens of Hamburg, 4,900 dead-weight on dimensions of 335.3 x 46.9 x 26.6, the "Moshulu" was launched as the "Kurt", along with a sister ship the "Hans", later to become the "Mary Dollar". Siemens ran the vessels in the South America trade coal out from Cardiff, Barry or Port Talbot with nitrate back to Britain or mainland Europe.

When the First World War broke out the "Kurt" was in Astoria on the American west coast and she was laid up until America entered the war in 1917 when the vessel was taken over, as a prize, by the US Shipping Board who renamed her "Dreadnought", however a little later all the German vessels seized by the United States were renamed by Mrs Woodrow Wilson, the President's wife, who with a degree of romantic whimsy gave them all Red Indian names, "Moshulu" meaning 'fearless'.

The Charles Nelson Company of San Francisco ran the vessel in the Pacific lumber trade to Australia until 1924 when she was laid up, in 1927 the "Moshulu" made one voyage and was again laid up in Seattle. Gustaf Erikson who had been interested in acquiring the vessel for twelve years bought the "Moshulu" from Nelson for $12,000, and Captain G. Boman took command. The "Moshulu" was then the largest sailing vessel afloat. With Captain G. HoIm in command the vessel left Gothenburg, in ballast,

"Moshulu" taken whilst in American ownership (R. Hogben collection)

on October 7th 1940, and reached Buenos Aires 55 days later. After loading maize she sailed for Denmark and was captured by the Germans in the North Sea, and taken to the Norwegian port of Farsund, the vessel spent the war years as a depot ship in various Norwegian ports. After the war she was laid up at Amsterdam and eventually was towed to Philadelphia where she serves as a museum/restaurant.

MOTOKETCH

In 1910 the "Motoketch" was launched at Millwall, London (see Traly), an auxiliary ketch of 78 x 20.2 x 9 and with a powerful engine which with the vessel's shallow draught made her ideal for the small ports of the Upper Bristol Channel. Around 1914 the "Motoketch" came to the Bristol Channel and was owned by a number of Bristol owners T. Jones, Mr. Plint and then B.A. Baker. The "Motoketch" became a familiar visitor to Bridgwater, Bristol and the Bay ports.

At the end of World War II the vessel was sold to French owners and was converted into a seaweed dredger and worked off the coast of Brittany.

"The Motoketch" as centrepiece to an evocative scene, Bristol before 1914.
Numerous small steam coasters and a P. and A.
Campbell paddle-steamer in the background (Author's collection)

MOZART

One of the more unusual vessels to use the Bay ports was the four mast barquentine "Mozart", built by the Grangemough and Greenock Dockyard Company at Greenock, launched in 1904, 2,003 tons with dimensions 262.9 x 40.1 x 24.2. The vessel was built for A.C. De Freitas of Hamburg and sold in 1911 to Schluler and Maack also of Hamburg, who used the vessel in the South American trade. In 1914 the vessel was in Taltal, Chile, and was interned until 1918 when she was allotted to the French. The vessel returned to Europe, under the French flag, in 1922, carrying a cargo of saltpetre from Taltal and arriving at Ostend in 93 days.

H. Lundquist, of Mariehamn, bought the vessel in 1922 attracted by the vessel's water ballast tanks which meant a saving on having to buy ballast, and the time wasted taking it on board and then unloading it. Lundquist used the vessel in the Australian grain trade until she was broken up in 1935.

In 1923 the "Mozart" left Melbourne on January 30th and arrived in Cardiff in June, having reached Queenstown after 181 days. The "Marlborough Hill" took 151 days Wallaroo to Queenstown then on to Cardiff. The average passage that year was 133.1 days. The "Mozart" left Port Victoria on March 3rd 1932, and arrived at Barry, via Falmouth, after 150 days. On February 1st 1933, the "Mozart" left Port Victoria and arrived in Cardiff via Falmouth for orders, in 113 days. Twenty vessels loaded grain that year and the average passage was 114.6 days. The vessel was scrapped in 1935.

"Mozart" (R. Hogben collection)

MUSKOKA

The "Muskoka", a steel four mast barque, crossing three sky sails, was regarded, as one of the fastest vessels of her day, and her master was Captain Albert Crow, a Nova Scotian, who was, "one of the best passage masters ever known". "Muskoka" was built by Richardson's of Stockton and launched in 1891 for F.C. Mahon of Nova

Scotia with a gross tonnage of 2,357 and dimensions of 300.5 x 42 x 24.7. For the First half dozen years of her life she took Welsh coal to China or Japan.

On January 25th 1898, she arrived at Queenstown from San Francisco after an excellent passage of 98 days, and was ordered to Cardiff to discharge her grain cargo. At Cardiff she loaded coal for the American fleet in the Far East, America was at war with Spain and the American fleet badly needed the best Welsh steam coal. Captain Crow "cracked on" and the "Muskoka" arrived at Hong Kong in 85 days, a quite extraordinary passage time. The "Renee Rickmers" arrived at Hong Kong from Barry in 93 days.

In 1908 the vessel was sold to A.D. Bordes and renamed "Caroline" and was lost in 1920, carrying coal to South America her cargo ignited, an all too common occurrence, and the vessel was beached at Antofagasta in July 1920.

"Muskoka" (R. Hogben collection)

NARCISSUS

R Duncan of Port Glasgow built the Narcissus a fully rigged iron ship of 1,336 tons with dimensions 235 x 37.1 x 22, and launched her in 1876 for Robert R Paterson and Company of Greenock, Scotland to be used in the sugar trade. A A Hurst described the ship as - "a striking vessel".

The "Narcissus" left Penarth on November 2nd 1883, with coal for India. Sailing without a second mate, there was continual trouble with the crew and the vessel put into Cape Town on January 18th 1884 when five men left the ship, one, Charles Ditton, being jailed. Five new crewmen were taken on and the vessel left on January 28th, arriving at Bombay on April 28. At Bombay the Mate and six crewmen paid off, Joseph Conrad, age 26, was signed on as Second Mate along with a new Mate and six crew. The vessel left for Dunkirk on June 3rd 1884 and arrived at Dunkirk after 136 days.

On September 24th when the ship was in the north Atlantic a member of the crew, a Negro, Joseph Barron aged 35 from Charlton County died. Reaching Dunkirk on October 16th all the officers and crew signed off.

Conrad based almost all his sea stories, characters and events on people and happenings from his life at sea, four members of the crew of the 'Narcissus" were drawn upon to appear in 'The Nigger of the Narcissus'. They were John Wild, AB of London, James Craig, AB of Belfast, Archie McLean, AB from Scotland and of course Joseph Barron. There were two Welshmen in the crew Evan Morgan aged 23, an AB from Cardiff and Tom Matthew, 19, an ordinary seaman from Newport. Given the "Narcissus" had sailed from Penarth and that there were two South Walians in the crew, it is possible that Conrad heard the Cutty Sark story on the "Narcissus".

The "Narcissus" was bought in 1889 by Captain Vittono Bartoletto of Camogli, Italy, who in 1916 sold the vessel to P Passos of Rio de Janeiro who re-named the vessel "Isis" under which name the vessel was in Baltimore in October 1921. The vessel sank in Rio in 1922, re-floated she was bought by E G Fontes and Co. and hulked in 1925.

Late in 1896 Joseph Conrad visited friends, the Spiridions, who resided at 78 Cathedral Road, Cardiff. When he arrived during December 1896 he had already had published 'Almayer's Folly' in 1895 and 'Outcast of the Islands' in 1896. Spiridion had helped finance the publication of the 'Outcast' (Fischer and Unwin) and was to be of further assistance to Conrad.

"Narcissus" the only known photograph of Joseph Conrad's best known vessel
(Author's collection)

Conrad arrived bearing the unfinished manuscript of the 'Nigger of the Narcissus'; he had been unable to produce an acceptable ending to the story. Spiridion furnished a special room where Conrad could work undisturbed. Jean Aubry in his biography of Conrad records-"concentration was exactly what Conrad wanted as he created the last and certainly most beautiful chapters of the story". Conrad later wrote in his 'Personal Record' that -"from his windows he could see the long tree lined street and on either side two identical terraces of neo-gothic villas".

On the 30th December 1896 he signed the Visitor's Book at Cardiff Central Library, then early in 1897 he wrote to his friend Edward Garnet, a reader at Fischer and Unwin-"the Nigger died on the 7th at 6pm".

NEW DESIGN

This vessel was one of the many sturdy ketches that plied their trade in the Bristol Channel, well into the twentieth century. The 'New Design" was built in Bridgwater by J Gough and launched in 1871 for C J Symons and Company of Bridgwater (see "Irene"). The vessel had a net reg. Tonnage of 50 tons with dimensions 74.2 x 18,1 x 7.9. When launched the vessel was a two-mast schooner and the Symons Company kept her in the East Coast of England trade, mainly between Hull and Aberdeen.

"New Design" sailing up an unidentified river towing what appears to be the vessel's punt and a hobbler's punt (R. Hogben collection)

When the vessel came back to the Bristol Channel she was converted into a ketch and was eventually bought by the colourful Appledore skipper, Captain James Screech. Up until the Second WW the vessel plied the Upper Channel in the coal trade, usually from Lydney or the Ely Tidal Harbour across to the English ports. Captain Screech often chartered to the firm of Lovering and Sons, ship owners and coal factors. The founder of the firm was John Lovering and one of his sons Arthur, one of the few remaining "Cardiff Dockmen" recently told me that he learnt to drive as a young boy driving his father's, Morris Cowley, back and fro at Lympsham Quay on the River Axe, taking the coal out of the hold of the "New Design". No doubt this was much appreciated by the crew of the ketch, it saved the hard work with the hand winch.

The "New Design" traded until the 1940's when the vessel was laid up at Bristol, where she rotted away.

NIVELLE

The "Nivelle" was launched in April 1897, by Scott of Greenock, who launched her sister ship, the more famous "Hougomont" in June 1897. The "Hougomont" was bought by Captain Gustaf Erikson in 1925 and was dismasted south of Cape Borda in 1932 becoming a breakwater at St. Vincent's Gulf South Australia.

The 'Nivelle' was of 2,430 tons with dimensions of 292.4 x 43.2 x 24.2 and was one of the many vessels that came to the Bay ports straight from the launching slip. The '"Nivelle" came from Greenock to Penarth and loaded coal for Montevideo making a passage of 56 days under Captain Williams. Under Captain Williams the vessel sailed to New York, Shanghai, Hongkong and various ports. Whilst taking coal from Newcastle, New South Wales, she was driven ashore and became a total loss on Point Grande, Antofagasta, on June 20th 1906

"Nivelle" as a new vessel (R. Hogben collection)

NORMA

The "Norma" was built in 1893 and launched by Barclay, Curle, and Co. for M.J. Begg of Cardiff, a steel four mast barque 2,122 gross tons with dimensions 278 x 41.2 x 24.1. She was a stump topgallant barque with a massive spread of canvas and was designed to carry an enormous cargo. She was brought straight from the launching slip by Captain D. McDonnell who took her on her maiden passage loaded with 3,500 tons of Welsh coal from Cardiff to Rio de Janeiro.

"Norma" under tow (R. Hogben collection)

Whilst discharging at Rio a revolution broke out, and the vessel came under cross fire, the hull was heavily marked by bullets and shrapnel, the crew constantly had to take refuge in the hold to escape flying bullets. One shell burst overhead and apiece weighing 2lbs was kept as a momento. None of the crew were hurt or killed, but a ballast lighterman was killed by a rifle bullet.

On April 20th 1907, whilst lying at anchor in the Semaphore Anchorage outside Adelaide, the "Norma" was rammed and sunk by the "Ardencraig", a steel full-rigger of 1,969 tons, built in 1886 by Russell's.

OLIVEBANK

Andrew Weir had no less than eight vessels added to his Bank Line, between 1891-2, and by 1895 had 25 vessels under his house-flag all the vessels ended their names with 'Bank'. Two of the vessels built between 1891-2 were the sister ships "Cedarbank" and the "Olivebank". The "Olivebank", launched in 1892, was a steel four mast barque of 2,824 tons with dimensions 326 x 43.1 x 24.5 and was built by Mackie and Thomson. Weir kept the "Olivebank" tramping until 1913 when the vessel was sold to E. Monson of Tredestrand, who renamed the vessel "Caledonia". Monson sold the vessel in 1916. Between 1913 and 1920 the vessel had five different Norwegian owners.

In 1924 the "Caledonia" left Geelong on May 28th and arrived at Cardiff via Queenstown, in 113 days, her last voyage under the Norwegian flag. Eleven vessels loaded in South Australia for Europe and the average passage was 124.3 days. After discharge Captain Walfrid Gustaffson came to Cardiff inspected the vessel and bought it for Captain Gustaf Erikson who renamed the vessel "Olivebank". The vessel left Cardiff in ballast under Captain K. Troberg and arrived in Port Lincoln, taking 106 days on passage. (In 1924 there were still about 250 large square-riggers afloat, not including deep-water barquentines and brigs).

On April 11th 1927, the "Olivebank" left Port Lincoln and arrived in Cardiff, via Queenstown, in 167 days, a very slow passage, losing two men in the heavy weather on the homeward passage. Seventeen vessels loaded and came home with a 131.9 days average passage. The best passage was made by the "Herzogen Cecilie", Port Lincoln to Hamburg via Queenstown, in 98 days. After unloading the "Olivebank" left Cardiff with a coal cargo for Luderitz Bay, arriving after 79 days.

The "Olivebank" left Melbourne on January17th 1931, and arrived in Cardiff, via Queenstown, in 122 days, fourteen vessels made the grain run with an average passage of 118 days. The best time being the beautiful "Herzogen Cecilie's", with the enigmatic Sven Erikson as master, an excellent passage of 93 days.

On March 20th 1939, the "Olivebank" left Port Victoria and arrived at Barry, via Queenstown, in 119 days. Thirteen vessels loaded in 1939 and averaged 124.5 days on passage, the best passage being the mighty "Moshulu", 91 days from Port Victoria to Glasgow.

After discharging at Barry the vessel left in September 1939, in ballast, to return to the Baltic and off Jutland in the North Sea on September 8th struck a German mine which blew the vessel's bottom out. The vessel's master captain Granith and 13 crewmembers were lost, seven being saved.

"Olivebank"
(R. Hogben collection)

PAMIR

The "Pamir" was a majestic four-mast barque of 3,020 tons launched by Blohm and Voss of Hamburg in 1905 for Laeisz of Hamburg, to join their large fleet of "P" liners. The vessel with dimensions of 316 x 46 x 26 was immediately put into the South American nitrate trade. Her best voyage up until the Great War was in 1906 under Captain C.N. Prentzmann - Isles of Scilly to Valparaiso 64 days and Iquique back to Scilly in 75 days.

The "Pamir" was interned during the Great War, 1914-1918, and at the end of hostilities allocated to the Italian Government, who ran her until 1924 when Laeisz, who was rebuilding his "P" line, bought her from the Italians for £7,000. In 1925 she made a smart passage out to Talcahuano from Hamburg in 75 days. Leaving Hamburg on December 20, 1925, experienced terrible weather in the English Channel on January 7th 1926 arrived at Falmouth having had several sails blown out, lost both her anchors and the starboard chain and having lost three men over-board.

Captain Gustaf Erikson bought the "Pamir" in 1931 for £4,000 and put her into the Australian grain trade, her first voyage under Captain J.M. Mattson was Wallaroo to London in 103 days. The vessel remained in the grain run until 1938 when she loaded guano for Auckland and then nickel ore, at Moumea, for Nordenhamn.

In 1939 "Pamir" left Port Victoria on March 8th and arrived at Southampton 96 days later, that year 13 square-riggers loaded grain for Britain with an average passage of 124 ½ days.

When the Second World War started the "Pamir" was in Gothenburg, she left on August 3rd 1940, to load guano at the Seychelles for Auckland and then re-turned for another load, 4,300 tons, which she unloaded at Wellington, New Zealand, in July 1941. Here the vessel was taken as a "War Prize" and the New Zealand Government put the vessel under the management of the Union S.S. Company.

The "Pamir" loaded wool and tallow for Bombay, however Japan's entry into the war forced the vessel to go to San Francisco, bringing grain back. During the war the "Pamir" made seven round trips, New Zealand to San Francisco or Vancouver. On her fifth voyage in 1944, Wellington to San Francisco on November12th in 24N, 146W, just north of Hawaii a large Japanese submarine surfaced and approached but then turned about and went away at high speed, perhaps the submarine commander thought the "Pamir" was a 'Q' ship!

After the war the "Pamir" made two more round trips to Vancouver, the vessel had made a profit of about £6,000 on average on the first seven voyages under the New Zealand flag, but a heavy loss on her two post-war voyages, after war-time freights had dropped.

In 1947 the vessel loaded and left Wellington under Captain H.S Collier, more familiarly known as "Two-Gun Pete", and reached London on December 22nd 1947, 80 days out from Wellington. After lying in the Shadwell Basin she was towed to Antwerp, loaded for Auckland and arrived after 109 days. On 12th November 1948 the vessel was handed back to Erikson and Captain Bjorkfelt resumed command.

On May 28th the "Pamir" left Port Victoria and arrived at Penarth, via Falmouth, a voyage of 127 days, the last commercial square-rigged sailing vessel to come around Cape Horn, the end of an epoch. The vessel was laid up at Penarth, a decision was taken to sell the vessel to the breakers but Herr Schliewen, a Hamburg ship-owner, bought the vessel and the "Pamir" was towed back to Germany arriving at Travemunde in January 1951. Auxiliary engines were installed plus radar and wireless. Schliewen ran the "Pamir" out and back to South America. In 1955 a consortium of German ship-owners bought the "Pamir", and the vessel was managed by Zerssen and Company of Rendsberg, her first voyage under Zerssen was cement from Hamburg to Beunos Aires.

In 1957, the "Pamir" was homeward bound having loaded a bulk cargo of grain at Buenos Aires, the loading having been done by soldiers the dockers being on strike. Overtaken by a hurricane, in mid-Atlantic, the cargo shifted, the vessel foundered and only six of the crew were saved, 80 perished.

Launch of the "Pamir" (Author's collection)

"Pamir" the beginning of the end. The "Pamir" leaving Port Victoria, 28th May,1949,
"Passat" in the background (Captain Henderson collection)

"Pamir, landfall approaching Falmouth, 2nd October, 1949, 127 days out
(Captain Henderson collection)

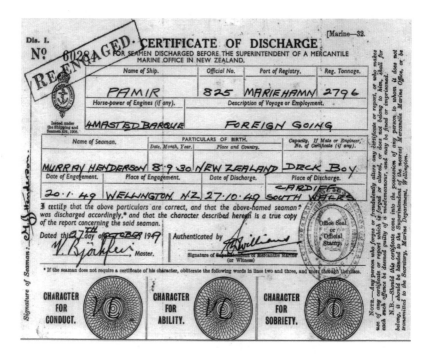

Murray Henderson's discharge certificate (courtesy of Captain Henderson who is secretary/treasurer of the New Zealand Pamir Association)

PARMA

In 1902 A. Rogers and Company of Glasgow launched a four-mast barque, the "Arrow", for the Anglo-American Oil Company. (This global company owned among many properties one large wooden wharf in the River Ely Tidal Harbour with seven storage tanks behind, it was later owned by Esso and was used by coastal tankers until the 1980s.) The vessel had a net tonnage of 2,882, gross 3,084 and could carry 5,300 tons on dimensions of 327.7 x 46.5 x 26.2. Initially the "Arrow" carried barrels of oil from New York to the Far East and Australia, then in 1912 Laeisz of Hamburg bought the vessel and renamed her "Parma". Between 1907 and 1914 Herr Laeisz bought 10 vessels, 4 British, 2 Italian and 4 German, five fully rigged ships and five barques and renamed them all with names beginning with the capital "P". The "Parma" was bought for £15,000.

At the start of the First World War all the Laeisz vessels were seized, the "Peiho" and the "Parma" were allocated to the British Government and managed for them by the General Steam Navigation Company. With the cessation of Hostilities Laeisz started to buy back his vessels and rebuild his "P" line. "Parma" was bought for £10,000 in 1921 and sailed for Delfzyl, from Chile, loaded with saltpetre that had been loaded in 1914. (In 1924 Laeisz bought back the Pamir for £7,000.) Laeisz put the "Parma" back in the South American nitrate trade, the "Parma's" last voyage for the "P" line was in 1930 the vessel left Iquique on June 8th and passed Pawle Point on April 12th . After discharging in Hamburg the vessel was laid up.

In 1931 the "Parma" was bought by a syndicate that included Captain Gustaf Erikson, Captain Rueben de Cloux and Alan Villiers, the vessel sailed from Hamburg in ballast in November 1931 under the command of Captain de Cloux. (De Cloux was born in 1884 and went to sea as a young boy and became a master mariner in 1909.) "Parma" reached Port Broughton, South Australia, on February 2nd 1932; the crew list shows de Cloux as Captain, three Finns as 1,2 and 3 mates. The crew was made up of 13 Finnish men, 7 German apprentices, 4 German men and a Finnish deck boy, Sven Caven of Abo. At Port Broughton the vessel loaded 5,220 tons, 62,650 bags all loaded by hand, sailed on March 18th and 103 days later anchored off Falmouth for orders to discharge at Cardiff. Nineteen vessels loaded in South America, one the "Melborne" was sunk, by collision, on the passage to Europe, the other 18 averaged 122.6 days on passage. Able Seaman Birger Stromberg remembered of the voyage: "It was the worst voyage I have ever been on, after about a month or so we were off the Horn. We had to sleep in the sail locker because everything was filled with water, we slept among the sails, and it was snowing..." After discharging the vessel sailed to Mariehanin.

The "Parma" made one more voyage under de Cloux, Elsinore to Port Victoria in ballast, Port Victoria to Hull, with a remarkable passage of 83 days via Falmouth for orders. Command of "Parma" now passed to de Cloux's brother-in-law Captain Karlsson who made three voyages in 1934, 1935 and 1936, Wallaroo to Birkenhead, Port Lincoln to Barry and the last voyage of the "Parma" Port Victoria to Glasgow, arriving at Falmouth in 117 days to be towed to Glasgow by the tugs "Warrior" and "Thunderer". After discharge the "Parma" was sold for £3,300 to the German ship breakers Kohlbrandwerft Paul Berendsohn.

"Parma" laid up at Hamburg, 1938, to be
scrapped (R.Hogben collection)

PASSAT

Blohm and Voss of Hamburg launched sister ships in 1911 the "Peking" and the "Passat" for Laeisz of Hamburg, the "Passat was of 3,183 tons, a large four mast barque with dimensions of 322 x 47.2 x 26.5. The vessel was employed in the South American trade and in 1914 seized as a War Prize and allocated to the French and spent 1914-1918 interned at Valparaiso, in 1921 Laeisz bought the vessel from the French and under Captain H. Ravn returned to Europe. From 1922 until 1932 Laeisz ran the "Passat" in the nitrate trade wherein she made numerous smart passages, e.g. in 1928 Tocopilla to Prawle Point, Devon, 71 days. However all was not plain sailing, in August 1928 the "Passat" left Hamburg on the 15th, off Dungeness a French steamer the "Daphe" tried to cross her bows, and was cut down and immediately sank. Fortunately the steamer's crew were saved, a year later on June 25th 1929, the "Passat" collided with a steamer " British Governer" in the English Channel off the Royal Sovereign LV.

In 1932 Gustaf Erikson bought the "Passat" for £6,500, she was lying at Bilbao after discharging her last cargo of nitrate. Under Captain G. Lindberg she was towed to Middlesborough and loaded fertiliser for Mauritius, where, after discharge she went to Assumption Island and loaded guano for Auckland.

Between 1933 and 1939 the "Passat" made seven grain runs from South Australia to Britain, to London, Dublin, Glasgow, Hull, Belfast and two passages to Barry. The "Passat" left Port Victoria on February 15th 1936 and arrived at Falmouth after 87 days, an excellent passage, and discharged at Rank's Mill, Barry Dock. Seventeen vessels loaded in 1936 with an average passage of 109 days. In 1937 the "Passat" loaded at Port Lincoln and left on February 18th taking 98 days to Falmouth, then onto Barry to discharge, both these good passages were made under Captain F. Gronland.

The "Passat" was in Mariehamn with the "Viking" and the "Pommern" when the Second World War started, the three vessels were towed to Stockholm and served as floating granaries then they were towed to Abo, Finland, loaded with supplies. After discharge at Abo the three Erikson barques were towed to Mariehamn and laid up.

In 1946 the "Passat" loaded timber in the Baltic and under the command of Captain Ivar Hagerstrand passed Elsinore on January 2nd 1947, arriving at East London, South Africa, 82 days later. (Duncan Carse, later to be Dick Barton on the BBC wireless, was a crewmember.) After discharge the vessel loaded 60,000 railway sleepers for Port Swettenham, (Malaya), then went to Port Victoria arriving in ballast on November 11th 1947.

"Passat" left Port Victoria on May 17th 1948 and reached Falmouth after 143 days, this very slow passage, carrying 4,547 tons of grain, was partially due to the vessel's foul bottom. After discharging at Avonmouth the "Passat" was towed to Port Talbot and loaded with sand and coal waste as ballast and sailed out to Port Victoria. After loading 55,000 sacks of grain the vessel left Port Victoria on June 2nd 1949 and arrived at Queenstown for orders on September 20th, a passage of 110 days.

Orders came on September 24th to sail to Penarth, anchor was weighed and the last commercial voyage by a large square-rigged sailing vessel began, and was well photographed by the Picture Post. The "Passat" was towed out from the roadstead and took seven days, tacking against an easterly wind, to reach Barry Roads. Anchored in the Roads the sails were taken in and given a fine "harbour stow" and a tug then towed the vessel to Penarth, docking on 2nd October 1949, a few days later the "Pamir" arrived having been towed from Falmouth.

The vessels lay at Penarth for some time and then were towed around to Barry for discharge, then returned to Penarth. In 1950 the "Passat" was bought by Herr Schliewen, as was the "Pamir", the "Passat" shared the same experiences as the "Pamir" until the last fateful voyage of 1957. The "Passat", badly loaded, left Buenos Aires sometime after the "Pamir", hit by high winds the vessel developed a dangerous list but was able to make Lisbon. Withdrawn from service, the Portuguese were keen to purchase the "Passat" for use as a training ship but they bought the "Guanabera" from Brazil, and the "Passat" was moored at Travemunde where she still lies.

The arrival of the "Pamir" and "Passat" at Penarth not only saw the end of an epoch the last oceanic voyages by large square-rigged vessels, but also saw the end of two very long careers in sail. Captain Verner Bjorkfelt had gone to sea as a young boy and had been a ship's master with Gustaf Erikson since 1933 in the "Killoran", 1933-1937, and the "Pamir" 1937-1949. Captain Ivar Hagerstrand had also gone to sea as a very young boy and had served as master on a number of Erikson's fleet, "Loch Linne", 1923-24, "Woodburn", 1924-25, "Hougomont", 1925-27, "Winterhude", 1928-29, "Viking", 1929-37 and the "Passat", 1945-49.

Launch of the "Passat" (Author's collection)

"Passat" in ballast leaving Auckland, New Zealand for Spencer Gulf, Australia
(R. Hogben collection)

"Passat" entering Penarth Dock
October 1949 (Author's collection)

"Pamir"and"Passat" Penarth Dock winter 1949/50.
(The foreground and background now totally destroyed and changed courtesy of the
Cardiff Bay Development Corporation). (Author's collection courtesy of Miss G. White)

Penarth Dock October 1949. The end of an epoch. The "Pamir" moored ahead of the
"Passat" at the end of the last two commercial voyages and roundings of Cape Horn by
square-rigged vessels.

PETER RICKMERS

In 1889 Russell and Company of the Clyde, built a vessel that can truly be described as a "tall ship". The "Peter Rickmers" was built for the famous firm Rickmers of Bremerhaven and was a four mast steel ship crossing four skysail yards above royals and double topgallants, and was considered by many to have been the most beautiful ship launched by Russell. The vessel was of 2,926 tons with dimensions of 332 x 44.4 x 25.4.

The vessel was towed, straight from the launch slip, to Cardiff in 1890, and loaded 4,468 tons of coal for Oleteh, Sumatra, arriving in 100 days. In 1894 the "Peter Rickmers" left Cardiff with 4,347 tons of coal for Singapore making a passage of 84 days, further voyages Cardiff to Singapore were made in 1895 and 1896. Between 1890 and 1906 the vessel also carried cargo to Bremen, Hong Kong, Antwerp and loaded at Rangoon, Astoria, New York. In 1907 the vessel loaded 4,303 tons of coal at Penarth for Singapore and made a passage of 95 days.

Unfortunately this handsome vessel went ashore on the coast of Long Island, USA, and became a total loss in 1908.

"Peter Rickmers" (R. Hogben collection)

PONAPE

The steel four-mast barque "Ponape" was launched at the yard of Soc Esercitzo Bacini, Genoa, for Pietro Milesi and Co. of Genoa in 1903. Launched as the "Regina Elena" the vessel was of 3,500 tons dead weight and her dimensions were 283.8 x 42.5 x 23.2. In 1911 Laeisz bought the vessel, and as a "P" liner renamed the vessel "Ponape". When the First World War broke out the barque was captured and taken into Falmouth as a War Prize and put with James Bell and Co. of Hull and renamed "Bellhouse" but sailed under the Norwegian flag, and in 1915 was acquired by A. Monsen of Tinsberg who managed her for the British. The famous Lancing whilst on a passage from Glasgow to Santos in 1921 sailed in company with the Bellhouse for two days and nights, extracts from a passenger's log record: ... "barque came near ... the Norwegian ship Bellhouse of Tonsberg, 46 days out of Sundersvall, Baltic with planking for Melbourne". And for January 15th: "she has steered more southerly and is out of sight".

On November 3rd 1925, Captain Hugo Lundquist and a group of friends bought the vessel and renamed her "Ponape"; the co-owners included a bank manager, eleven other Master Mariners including Reuben de Cloux, seven farmers and various others. They all held a share measured in l00ths, for example Lundquist 35/100, de Cloux 2/100, Farmer Axel Karlsson 2/100.

The vessel was placed in the Australian grain trade. In 1925 Captain Gustaf Erikson sent Captain Hagerstrand (see "Passat") to inspect the vessel but thought the asking price of £6,000 too high, then in 1929 the "Ponape" left Geelong, South Australia and arrived at Falmouth on August 6th and was ordered to Cardiff, after discharging the vessel lay in Cardiff and Gustaf Erikson sent Captain Uno Karlssen to inspect the vessel which Erikson bought for *£5,500*. The "Ponape" left Cardiff on September 17th and arrived at Port Lincoln on December 12th with Captain Uno Karlssen in command.

Under Erikson's houseflag, the "Ponape" made another six grain runs from South Australia to Rotterdam, Glasgow and four to London, her last voyage was in 1936 leaving Port Germein in February and reaching London in June, after unloading the vessel was laid up in London until the end of September when the vessel was sold to the breakers for £3,425. Her figurehead was saved and is in the Aland Maritime Museum in Mariehamn.

"Ponape" cracking along, all sail set (R. Hogben collection)

QUEEN MARGARET

McMillan launched a four-mast barque, crossing skysail yards on three masts over royals, the "Queen Margaret" was considered by most "experts" to have been one of the most beautiful and fastest vessels of the 1890s. The vessel was launched in 1893 for John Black and Co, 2,144 tons with dimensions of 275 x 42.2 x 24 and her first commander was a 6 foot 4 inch Nova Scotian, Captain D. F. Faulkner who was remembered as "a splendid windjammer seaman".

The vessel's third voyage started at Cardiff on March 30th 1896, carrying 3,390 tons of Welsh coal for Nagasaki arriving there after 119 days, the freight was £2,627. On April 9th 1897, the vessel left Liverpool and arrived at Barry, under tow, on April 11th, the vessel was then towed to Cardiff, dry docked and had her bottom painted. The "Queen Margaret" left Barry on April 30th loaded with 3,360 tons of coal and arrived at Nagasaki after 103 days, freight £3,198.

On April 3rd 1898, the "Queen Margaret" left Dunkirk in ballast, under tow, and arrived in Cardiff on April 6th, the vessel was then dry-docked and its bottom cleaned and painted. On June 17th she left Cardiff for New York in ballast, arriving on July 29th, in New York the vessel loaded 88,000 cases of oil for Hong Kong, arriving on March 5th, 1899. From 1899 until 1912 the vessel traded worldwide and visited, among other ports, Antwerp, San Francisco, Tacoma, Shanghai. In July 1912 the vessel was in Barry, leaving on July 25th, for Montevideo. On January 17th 1913, the "Queen Margaret" left Sydney with 4,500 tons of wheat and arrived off the Lizard at daybreak on May 5th 108 days out. Here Captain Bousfield received orders to proceed to Limerick, at 8 o'clock the vessel struck rocks and stuck fast. The Lizard lifeboat arrived and took off Mrs Bousfield and her young son, the ship's company followed in their own boats and the "Queen Margaret" broke up.

"Queen Margaret" (R. Hogben collection)

R.C. RICKMERS

This massive five mast auxiliary barque was built by Rickmers at Bremerhaven and launched in 1906; she was of 5,548 gross tons on dimensions of 410.5 x 53.6 x 30.4 and could load up to 7,500 tons. The vessel's engine was of 1,000 bhp and could push her along at 7 knots loaded and 8 knots unloaded, the total cost of the vessel was £75,000. During the vessel's first ten years she traded globally and visited many ports including Antwerp, Hamburg, Kobe, Rangoon and Singapore and carried various cargoes, e.g. caseoil, cement, coal, rice, wheat etc.

In 1914 the vessel loaded 6,880 tons of beans and hemp seed at Vladivostok and arrived at Hull after a 98 day passage, whilst unloading at Hull the First World War started and the vessel was seized as a Prize of War by the British Government and renamed "Neath". When on passage from Gambo, Newfoundland to Cardiff, the vessel stranded on Beachie's head, Alexander Bay, Newfoundland, fortunately the barque was re-floated with only minor damage and preceded to Cardiff. Unfortunately the vessel did not last long, being sunk, ironically, by a German submarine.

"R.C.Rickmers" photographed during the First World War as the "Neath" (W.I.M.M.)

RENEE RICKMERS

A four masted barque built by Russell's of Port Glasgow in 1887 for the Rickmer's of Bremen, the "Renee Rickmers" was 3,300 tons dead weight, gross tonnage 2,135 tons and net tonnage 2,054 tons. Her dimensions were 283 x 40.5 x 24.6. The vessel traded from South Wales to the west coast of South America and to Australia. In 1913 she loaded Australian grain and was homeward bound when Gustaf Erikson put in a bid for the vessel of £6,500 pending a hull inspection.

On October 26th 1913, the vessel arrived at Falmouth and accepted orders for Cardiff. After being towed to Cardiff the vessel was discharged and then dry-docked where she was inspected by Captain M. Nordberg. The vessel was fitted out, on credit, by the Cardiff ship chandler Charles Huss and the vessel was renamed "Aland".

The "Aland" loaded coal for Callao and left Cardiff on January 11th 1914 and arrived at the South American port after a passage of 113 days, after unloading she sailed in ballast to New Caledonia to load nickel ore for Europe. Approaching her destination she ran onto a reef on August 20th 1914 and was wrecked.

"Renee Rickmers" later re-named "Aland" (Aland Sjofartsmuseum)

RESULT

This fine three mast double topsail schooner of 122 gross tonnage on dimensions 102 x 21.7 x 9.1 was built by Paul Rodgers of Carrickfergus, Belfast Lough, and completed by R. Kent and Company in January 1893 for Thomas Ashburner of Barrow-in-Furness. Her early trading was mainly Welsh slate from the then busy port of Porthmadog to Hamburg until 1909 when she was bought by a group of Braunton men including G.C. Clark and Captain Incledon. With Captain Incledon in command the vessel went to Antwerp with white bricks from Bideford and carried cargoes around the British coast and to France e.g. Newhaven, Morlaix, etc.

An engine was installed in 1914 and in 1916 the vessel was taken to Lowestoft and fitted out as a "Q" ship, being equipped with two 12 pounders and two torpedo tubes. The vessel as HMS "Result" engaged the U-45 in Action, on February 15th 1917, and was in action again on April 4th 1917, with another U-boat during which the "Result" sustained damaged plates.

The vessel was "de-mobbed" in August 1917 and resumed trading to French ports and other ports between Brest and the Elbe. During the early 1920s, her upper topsail yard was removed and in 1925 Captain Tom Welsh left the ketch "Democrat" to become master of the "Result", and it was about this time that her remaining topsail yard was removed and she sailed as a plain for and aft schooner. The vessel traded through the Second World War and in 1946 a bigger 120-hp engine was installed. In 1950 she was restored to her original glory, re-rigged as a topsail schooner to play the part of Captain Lingard's schooner "Flash" in a film version of Conrad's "Outcast of the Islands", with the late lamented Trevor Howard as the leading man.

In the early 1950's the vessel's main hatch was enlarged and the mainmast removed. The "Result" continued trading as an auxiliary ketch with Captain Peter Welch in command having taken over from his father. The "Result" carried on trade mainly with the Channel Islands.

The "Result" traded into the 1960's and her activities were well recorded in the Sea Breezes, e.g. October 1960: "The Result traded between the Channel Islands and south coast ports carrying miscellaneous cargoes. In August she loaded 160 tons of agricultural lime at Littlehampton for Jersey, then a cargo of stone from Guensey to Shoreham Harbour, followed by a trip in ballast to the Thames where she loaded cement at Northfleet for the Channel Islands." The December issue of 1960 reported: "During the Autumn the Result has taken several stone cargoes from Jersey to Shoreham with lime on return, at the end of August she had varied this routine by running a coal cargo from Cardiff to the small Cornish port of Portreath". In the July 1964 issue of the Sea Breezes it reports: "The former schooner Result continues her usual Channel Isles trade from Littlehampton and other south coast ports".

The "Result's" August 1960 visit to Cardiff Bay appears to have been the last occasion a sailing vessel loaded in a Bay port.

The "Result" continued trading until 1967 when she was withdrawn from trade on the death of her owner/skipper Captain P. Welch. The vessel is now at the Ulster Folk and Transport Museum at Cultra, Northern Ireland.

"Result" in her middle-age as a three mast motorised schooner, minus her yards and square- sails (Ulster Folk and Transport Museum)

"Result" at Exeter at the end of her long career, reduced to a motorised ketch
(Ulster Folk and Transport Museum)

"Result" re-rigged to her original rig as a three mast, square top-sail schooner to play
Conrad's "Flash" *c.*1950 (Ulster Folk and Transport Museum)

RICKMER RICKMERS

The Rickmers of Bremen were one of Germany's greatest ship owners as well as being shipbuilders, millers and importers. The "Rickmer Rickmers" was launched by the firm on July 27th 1896 and took to the water at Bremerhaven, a steel full rigged ship of 1,980 tons gross; unusually for the period she had large tanks to hold 1,000 tons of water ballast. The 264 foot vessel was towed to Cardiff, to make her maiden voyage, a cargo of coal for Saigon with a rice cargo home. After sustaining damage in 1904 she put into Cape Town and was rigged down to a barque.

In 1912 she was sold to a Hamburg firm C. Krabbenhoft and Bock and renamed "Max" and joined the large fleet of vessels engaged in the Chilean nitrate trade. On June 23rd 1914, she left Caleto Coloso with nitrate for Hamburg, in the Atlantic a passing vessel signalled that the First World War had started so the Captain put into a neutral port Horta in the Azores. The vessel then was taken over by the Portuguese Government, discharged, and then renamed "Flores" and traded until the 1920's slump when she was laid up.

The Portuguese navy acquired the vessel in 1924 and converted her to a school-ship, a role she fulfilled until 1961, renamed "Sagres", in this role she participated in the early Sail Training Races. In 1962 the vessel was renamed "Santo Andre" and became a stationary depot ship.

In about 1982 the vessel was purchased by a German syndicate and towed from Lisbon to Hamburg and restored, she now serves as a museum ship and restaurant, having been completely restored and fitted out, between 1984-86, including being given a new figurehead of Rickmer Rickmers as a young boy, dressed in the national dress of Heligo land.

"Rickmer Rickmers" lying at Hamburg *c.* 1990 (R. Hogben collection)

"Rickmer Rickmers" (R. Hogben collection)

RYELANDS

A wooden three mast double topsail schooner built at Glasson Dock in 1887, a vessel of 158 tons with dimensions of 102.2 x 22.9 x 10.8, she traded as a slater carrying North Wales slate to the continent and ran regularly in the Cornish china clay trade from the small Cornish ports, usually to Connah's Quay. In 1931 her topsail yards were discarded and an engine installed.

In December 1942 Captain Shaw of Gloucester bought the "Ryelands" and his son Captain Humphrey K. Shaw relinquished the command of the "Irene" and took charge of the schooner. Both the Ryelands and the Camborne spent the rest of the Second World War trading in the Bristol Channel, where they both became familiar sights in the Bay ports, usually carrying cargoes, discharged from large steamers at Avonmouth, to the smaller ports of the Bristol Channel and from the Bay to the English ports. But neither vessel went further south than Penzance or Hayle. In 1946 Captain Shaw sold both vessels.

In the 1950s the schooner took part in films, first as the Hispaniola in "Treasure Island" and then suitably altered and renamed "Pequod" for the film Moby Dick. As the "Pequod" she came into Cardiff in 1950 towed by two tugs, the "King's Cross" and the "Standard Rose".

The "Sea Breezes", December 1960, reported that the film ship 'Neptune', ex-"Ryelands" arrived at Morecombe from Falmouth owned by Peter Latham, to be used as a floating cafe"'. Earlier in the "Sea Breezes", October 1959, F. Jones of Norwich who had sailed in the in the "Ryelands" wrote that, "she was very dry on deck in bad weather ... a good all round sailer".

"Ryelands" at Appledore 1945
(B.Greenhill collection)

"Ryelands" converted to the "Pequod" for the film 'Moby Dick', being towed into Cardiff c.1950 by the tugs "Kings Cross" and "Standard Rose" (W.I.M.M.)

"Ryelands" in the Bute East Dock, Cardiff as the "Pequod" *c.*1950
(T. Morgan Collection)

SENATOR

The "Senator" was built by Mounsey and Foster of Sunderland for T and S Harrison, launched in May 1874, an iron ship crossing a main sky sail yard this "tall ship" was of 1,695 tons with dimensions of 256.2 x 41.1 x 23.6. In 1889 the "Senator" went from Cardiff to San Francisco in 90 days, a record for an iron ship, bettering the "Merioneth's" so called 'record' by six days. Soon after the record run Harrison's sold the vessel to J R de Wolf who sold her to Brazilian owners in 1910.

SIERRA SHIPPING COMPANY

John Masefield immortalised the "Sierras" for their good looks, with white hulls they were always kept smart and clean. Their fleet contained fourteen vessels, all iron or steel three or four masters, all built between 1875-1889, most of whom visited the Bay ports. Here are a few examples.

"Sierra Blanca" launched by Scott's of Greenock in 1875, the vessel was of 1,518 tons with dimensions of 249.4 x 38 x 23.3. In 1897 the vessel sailed from Penarth to Mauritius in 62 days, a record for this passage, the vessel eventually ended up under the Norwegian flag, re-rigged as a barque.

The "Sierra Cadena" was built by T. Royden and Sons and launched in 1884. The vessel was of 1,855 tons with dimensions of 268.1 x 42.1 x 24. When launched the vessel was named "Calistoga" and renamed when bought by the Sierra Line. In 1899 the "Sierra Cadena" sailed from Penarth to Mauritius in 75 days. The vessel was sold and re-named "Prince George", being broken up in 1925.

Richards and Duck launched the "Sierra Colonna" in 1878, an iron fully rigged ship of 1,435 tons on dimensions of 238.6 x 38 x 22.8, in 1900 she sailed from Penarth to Mauritius in 74 days. The vessel was eventually sold to the Norwegians.

The "Sierra Lucena" was built by Robert Steele in 1883 as the "Inveruglas" for Milne, after one voyage the vessel was sold to Thompson, Anderson and Co. founders of the Liverpool Sierra Line, and renamed "Sierra Lucena". The vessel was an iron ship of 1,684 tons, 260.4 x 39 x 23.5. During 1900 the vessel loaded coal at Penarth for Mauritius, arriving after a passage of 76 days. In 1904 the vessel was bought by the Norwegians and renamed "Sophie" by her new owner Charles Nielsen. He sold the vessel to American owners in 1923 who ran her as the "Tusitala" between Baltimore, Seattle and Honolulu. Laid up in 1937, the vessel was broken up in 1938.

In 1884 J. Reid and Company launched a steel three mast full rigged ship, the "Sierra Miranda", 1,808 tons with dimensions of 264.7 x 39.1 x 23.9. During 1897 the vessel left Penarth and made a good passage of 67 days to Mauritius. In 1907 she was sold to Norwegian owners in Stavanger and cut down to a barque, changing hands several times she ended up in 1922 under the Panamanian flag owned by Brown Willis and as such sank at her moorings in 1922.

"Sierra Lucena" as the "Tutsitala" in an American port *c.*1930's (P. Rundle collection)

SPRINGBURN

In 1894 Barclay, Curle launched the "Springburn", a steel four mast barque of 2,655 tons gross on dimensions of 290 x 45.6 x 25.7 for Shankland's Burn Line to be used in the jute trade, however her maiden voyage was out to the American west coast with a grain cargo from San Francisco on return. In 1895 the vessel left Cardiff and arrived at Cape Town in 37 days, this on her way out to Newcastle, New South Wales.

In 1896 the "Springburn's" apprentices kidnapped one of San Francisco's most notorious crimps, "Shanghai Brown", and earned undying fame by 'selling' him to an outward bound skipper, thus sending Brown on a winter's passage around Cape Horn.

The vessel was sold in 1906 to A.D. Bordes who renamed her "Alexandre", the vessel being torpedoed and sunk in the First World War.

"Springburn" (R. Hogben collection)

SPRINGBANK

Russell's of Port Glasgow launched the "Springbank, a four mast steel barque of 2,398GRT on dimensions of 282.4 x 43 24.4 for Andrew Weir's Bank Line in 1894. (In 1895 Weir owned 25 vessels which had increased to 30 by 1900 and this did not include his 11 steam vessels). On one voyage the vessel left Melbourne, loaded with grain, and arrived at Queenstown for orders in 90 days, an excellent passage. After a few days anchored at Queenstown the "Springbank" was towed to Cardiff and discharged. There were several French vessels, full rigged ships and barques, awaiting their turn to load so it was four weeks before the "Springbank" started to load coal for Antofagasta.

Whilst loading a new crew were signed on, the sail maker was an old Montenegrin and the carpenter was a young Sid Wright, who later established the Cardiff Boat Building Company and who built for himself the beautiful yacht "Corisande", which for years was 'Cock of the Channel'. Four new apprentices were signed on and most of the crew were Finns. When the vessel reached Antofagasta there were about thirty sailing vessels in the roadstead, most of whom had loaded coal in the Bristol Channel. In 1919 the vessel was bought by E. Monsen of Tvedestrand and was renamed "Asrym" and had several Norwegian owners before being lost in the 1920s on a passage from Newport News, USA, to Aalborg.

"Springbank" (Author's collection)

SOUTHERN BELLE

This wooden three mast barque of 587 tons gross with dimensions of 146 x 31.4 x 18.8 was built in Digby, Nova Scotia by J. Mulcaha in 1871 and was owned by A.C. Robbins, a well-established ship owner and grocer of Yarmouth, Nova Scotia. The vessel traded up and down the eastern seaboard of the Americas and was in Florida in the 1880s. In 1889 a group of Finns acting through a Cardiff shipbroker bought the vessel for £2,050 and under the command of Captain Matts Robert Widlund the vessel loaded coal at Cardiff for La Plata. In 1890 the vessel still under Captain Widlund and with a young Gustaf Erikson as Konstapel loaded coal at Cardiff for Dakar.

Gustaf Erikson went to sea, at the age of ten, as a cabin boy, on the barque 'Neptun" with Captain K. Eriksson in command and made a voyage of 4 months and 3 days leaving Aland on May 14th 1883. Later on April 14th 1885, he left Aland as the cook on the barquentine Adele skippered and owned by his father Gustaf Adolf, a voyage of 3 months 15 days.

The "Southern Belle" arrived in Cardiff with Baltic timber from Hernosand on June 3rd 1904, the vessel was also in Newport in 1903 and Swansea in 1904 and 1905.

Gustaf Erikson became owner of the Southern Belle in 1917 and in 1919 the vessel was sold to the ship breakers, her masts and rigging being saved and used to rig the "Carmen", a three mast wooden barque, launched in 1921. Erikson acquired the "Carmen" in 1924. Between 1913 when Erikson bought his first vessel the three-mast barque "Tjerimai" until his death in 1947 he owned some 46 large sailing vessels and had shares in many others, e.g. "Parma", he also owned or had interests in numerous fully powered steam and motor vessels.

"Southern Belle" flying the Finnish flag in 1919 (Aland Sjofartsmuseum)

TERPSICHORE

A fine iron full rigged ship with deep single topgallants built in 1883 by Royden's of Liverpool for B. Wenke and Sohne of Hamburg, the vessel was of 2,025 gross tons. The vessel's first voyage was to Mauritius and she was badly damaged by a cyclone in the Indian Ocean.

The vessel was in Cardiff in 1893 and left on April 25th loaded with coal for South America. She left Cardiff in company with the "Valkyrie", both vessels being towed down to Lundy Island by the tugs "Black Cock" and "Storm Cock" respectively.

At the outbreak of the First World War the "Terpsichore" was discharging grain at Limerick, Ireland, and was seized by the British Government as a War Prize and was then run by the British Shipping Controller under the management of R, Thomas, she made a number of Atlantic crossings. After the war the vessel was put into the South Australian trade.

On September 10th 1921, the vessel left Sydney and arrived at Queenstown for orders docking at Cardiff on January 31st 1922, a long passage of 143 days. Sixty-eight sailing vessels loaded grain in Australia in 1921 for Europe, with an average passage of 131.4 days. The quickest passage was the "Marlborough Hill" 91 days from Port Lincoln to Cardiff, the slowest being the Desaix 202 days Port Lincoln to Sunderland.

After discharging at Cardiff the vessel was laid up, most probably on the West Mud and was sold in 1922 for only £250, then towed to Gibraltar ending up as a coal hulk at that port.

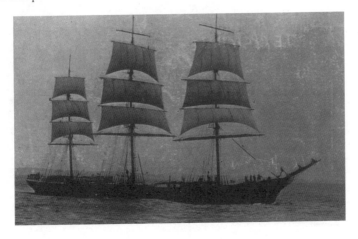

"Terpsichore" (R. Hogben collection)

TERRA NOVA

A whaler built at Dundee by Alex Stephen in 1884, she spent many years whaling and sealing in Greenland waters. In 1901 Captain Robert Falcon Scott went to the Antarctic on the "Discovery", a research vessel built on whaler lines, although larger, and launched by Alex Stephen in 1901. Between 1901 - 1904 Scott surveyed the Great Ice Barrier and the "Terra Nova" was chartered by the British Government to go to the relief of the "Discovery". On returning from the Antarctic the "Discovery" was sold to the Hudson Bay Company as a cargo vessel.

In June 1910 the "Terra Nova", a barque rigged steam auxiliary, left Cardiff, taking Scott's party to the Antarctic, Scott left the vessel off the Breaksea Lightship, and returned to Cardiff on the aptly named tug "Falcon", accompanied by the Lord Mayor of Cardiff and a party of ladies and gentlemen. Scott rejoined the "Terra Nova" to sail to the Antarctic, at Port Lyttelton, New Zealand. In 1913 the "Terra Nova" made a sombre return to Cardiff. The "Discovery" is moored on the Thames Embankment, London.

"Terra Nova" leaving Cardiff June 15th 1910.
Note the Lord Mayor's party on the aft deckhouse (W.I.M.M.)

TILKHURST

A full rigged iron sailing ship of 1,527 tons built by A. McMillan and Sons of Dumbarton, in 1877, for W.R. Price and Co. of London.

The vessel left Hull, in ballast, on April 24th 1885, under the command of Captain E.J. Blake with twenty-six officers and crew, and Joseph Conrad, 27, as second mate. The "Tilkhurst" arrived at Penarth on May 14 to load coal for Singapore, leaving Penarth on June 10th and arriving at Singapore, on September 22nd.

On the eve of leaving Singapore, a drunken quarrel broke out among the crew, fighting began and William Cumming, 23, an able seaman from Bristol sustained a heavy blow to the head and became delirious: as the vessel moved through the Malacca Strait he jumped overboard. Conrad combined the deaths of Cummings and Barron on the "Narcissus" to use in "The Nigger of the Narcissus". The character Singleton in that story was based on Daniel Sullivan who was an able seaman on the "Tilkhurst".

In 1893 the "Tilkhurst" was sold to the famous French ship owning firm A.D. Bordes et Fils and renamed "Blanche" and who for ten years ran her as a nitrate carrier. Bordes, as well as having vessels built for them, also bought 14 British vessels, including the "Tilkhurst". In 1903 the vessel was acquired by G. Mortola of Genoa and was eventually broken up at Genoa in 1923, a year before Conrad's death.

Conrad sailed in 15 sailing vessels and 4 steam vessels, his sailing vessels included the "Otago" and the "Torrens". One of his steamers was the small "Mavis" of 764 tons, Conrad signed on as an ordinary seaman in Marseilles, April 24th 1879. Two years later, on November 24th 1880, the "Mavis" struck rocks off Ile d'Oleron, France whilst on a passage from Cardiff to Bordeaux with coal. The vessel was lost and two crewmen drowned.

"Tilkhurst". The vessel appears to have taken the ground in the narrow dredged channel leading to Cardiff and Penarth Docks. The green hills of Somerset can be seen in the background (R. Hogben collection)

TRALY

The "Traly" was one of the last trading ketches built in the UK, launched in 1912 by Edwards and Co., Millwall, London, complete with an 80 bhp engine, she was a steel vessel of 108 gross tons on dimensions of 79.7 x 20.1 x 9.0 and was built for Irish owners based at Tralee, County Kerry, who ran her in the Irish Sea trades, bricks, coal, oats, timber etc. The vessel had a hinged bowsprit to reduce her length in dock.

Just after the end of the First World War the vessel was bought by G. Clarke of Braunton who used her in the brick trade mainly Bridgwater to Liverpool. In 1936 Clarke sold the "Traly" to W.H. Petherick and Sons of Bude who used her to carry coal into Bude usually from Lydney or the Bay Ports.

During the 1950s the "Traly" could regularly be seen making smoky diesel passages between the Ely Harbour and Avonmouth with bunker coal.

In April 1958 the vessel was sold to Captain N.H. Ammersboll of Copenhagen and left Appledore on May 2nd, to load coal at Swansea before leaving for the Baltic. Ammersboll renamed the vessel "Karna" and used her in general trade in the Baltic. In October 1965 the vessel ran aground whilst bound to load fertiliser (see Charlotte Rhodes). Some years later the "Traly" was sold to Christian Duehoim Patrederm who converted her into a gravel and sand dredger, based at Temmerstrand on the Jutland peninsular, and she was renamed "Ral". The "Ral" worked until 1991 when she was scrapped.

"Traly" entering Bude, hobbler's punt alongside (Bude Museum)

"Traly", an excellent photograph of the vessel in the sea-lock at Bude.
The spectator's mode of dress suggests *c.*1930's (Bude Museum)

"Traly" in the harbour at Bude moving to the un-loading berth (Bude Museum)

"Traly" at Appledore in 1946 awaiting survey minus her bowsprit
(B. Greenhill collection)

ULRICH

The "Ulrich" was built and launched as the "Mozambique" in 1892 by Russell for J. Boyd of Glasgow, a four mast steel barque of 2,145 tons gross with dimensions of 283.3 x 43 x 24.2. Boyd ran the vessel in general trading including coal from Cardiff Bay, in 1912 the vessel was sold to the Germans, Wm. Miller of Hamburg who loaded coal at Cardiff for the Chilean nitrate ports.

Returning to Hamburg with nitrate from Chile the "Ulrich" was captured on October 20th 1914, by the HMS Venus and was sold by the War Prize Court to the Norwegians in 1915. Owned by S.O. Stray the vessel was abandoned in a sinking condition on March 5th 1920, on a passage from Norfolk, USA, to Montevideo, there were some survivors but thirteen of the crew drowned.

"Ulrich" ex-"Mozambique" (R. Hogben collection)

VICTORINE

The "Victorine" was a smart wooden ship of 1,621 tons built at Bordeaux in 1858 for the highly successful French firm of A.D.Bordes. This "Victorine" must not be confused with Bordes' later iron ship, also "Victorine", built by Stephen of Dundee who also built the "Terra Nova".

Antonin Dominique Bordes went to Chile in 1835, there he met Captain Le Quellac and they started a ship-owning partnership. Le Quellac became a 'sleeping partner 'in 1845. Bordes returned to France in the 1860s on board his own "Victorine" along with his pregnant wife, two daughters and three sons. The "Victorine" usually took general cargo and passengers from Bordeaux to Valparaiso, loading nitrate back usually to British ports. Then in 1870 Bordes imported the first cargo of nitrate into France for the benefit of French agriculture, and soon established nitrate depots at Dunkerque, Nantes, La Rochelle and Bordeaux.

Between 1845 and 1935 Bordes owned a total of 127 sailing vessels and from 1880 usually had between thirty and forty in commission at any one time. The other major European company, in the nitrate trade Laeisz of Hamburg owned 80 vessels between 1856 and the 1930s, but never had more than fifteen in commission at any given time.

The "Victorine" was in Penarth in 1865 and the Cardiff Times of November 30th 1865, reported: "Baptiste Peret of the "Victorine" fell into the dock and drowned". The Inquest was held at the Cogan Hotel, Cogan, Penarth and Peret is buried in St. Augustine's Churchyard, Penarth. The vessel was lost in 1875.

VIKING

In 1907 Burmeister Wain of Copenhagen launched the "Viking", a steel four mast barque for Handes Foades Skolskit Bafalingsmaend, the vessel was of 2,952 tons with dimensions of 293.8 x 45.9 x 23.8 and was built as a commercial carrier and sail-training vessel. When the First World War started the vessel was laid up, and in 1916 she was bought by the Danish United Steamships Co. of Copenhagen and put into the South Australian grain trade. In 1921 the vessel sailed from Sydney to Bordeaux in 107 days and was again laid up. During 1923 the vessel was put back into commission and went from Geelong to Antwerp in 119 days in 1924. In 1925 the "Viking" went from Port Victoria to Rotterdam in a very slow passage of 149 days and was again laid up. During 1927 she went out to Callao via Barbados and returned with guano to be laid up yet again.

In 1929 Gustaf Erikson bought the "Viking" for £6,500, having been neglected whilst laid up, her hold was a mass of rust and she needed a suit of new sails, to remedy these shortcomings cost Erikson another £3,000. The vessel was sailed from Copenhagen to Mariehamn by Captain Reuben de Cloux. The vessel's first commercial voyage under Erickson's houseflag was timber from Hernosand to

Australia commanded by Captain Ivar Hagerstrand (see "Passat"), he was to remain in command until 1937.

On February 8th 1932, the "Viking" left Port Victoria and arrived in Cardiff, via Queenstown in June. Nineteen sailing vessels loaded Australian grain that year, 18 came to the U.K., one went to Rotterdam with an average passage of 122.6 days.

In 1934 the "Viking" left Port Victoria and arrived at Barry via Falmouth.

On February 16th, 1939, the "Viking" left Port Victoria commanded by Captain Uno Morn and arrived at Cardiff after having taken orders at the Lizard. Thirteen vessels loaded grain for the UK, ten belonged to Erikson, the average passage for the thirteen was 122 days. The best passage was the "Moshulu", 91 days, the slowest passage being the "Lawhill", 140 days to Glasgow. The "Viking" left Cardiff in ballast and was at Mariehamn when the Second World War started and she spent the war as a storage vessel.

After the war the "Viking" loaded Baltic timber and commanded by Captain KarlBroman, who had been Master of Erikson's large 4,050 ton "Pommern" from 1933–1939, passed Elsinore, outward bound on December 31st 1946, and arrived at East London, South Africa, after a passage of 93 days. After unloading, the vessel loaded coal for Santos, Brazil and then sailed in ballast for South Australia. On March 11th 1948, the "Viking" left Port Victoria on March 11th and docked at London. The "Viking" was laid up and in 1950 was bought by the town of Gothenburg and towed there in 1951, the vessel is now open to the public at Gothenburg.

"Viking" under the Danish flag (R. Hogben collection)

"Viking", Queen Alexandra Dock, Cardiff, 1939. Penarth Head in background, Breton
schooner right background (W.I.M.M.)

WANDERER

W.H. Potter and Co. of Liverpool built the "Wanderer" at their own Liverpool
yard and the vessel was launched on August 20th 1891. The vessel was of 2,903
tons on dimensions 309 x 46 x 25.8 and could carry 4,500 tons. The four-mast barque
crossed skysail yards on her fore and main masts. Many hold that the "Wanderer"
was the finest of the many big sailing vessels launched in the decade 1890-1899.
The poet John Masefield wrote numerous poems about the "Wanderer" and lines
included: "At night the verdict left my messmates lips ... The Wanderer is the finest
ship in the dock." .."The Wanderer, clipper, outward bound, the loveliest ship my
eyes have ever seen ... "You swept across the waters like a Queen". Basin Lubbock
wrote that she was: "in truth a beautiful ship."

The vessel was launched at 11.38 am on August 20th 1891, and on August 26th
she was moved into the Queen's Half-tide Dock to be rigged. On Saturday, September 12th she was towed across the river to Birkenhead and there loaded Westmin-
ster Brymbo Steam coal for San Francisco.

The vessel sailed on October 17th 1891 under Captain George Currie, a Nova
Scotian, and with John Masefield as an apprentice. Masefield, who became Poet
Laureate in 1930, had joined HMS Conway, as a twelve year old boy, when she lay
in the Mersey off Liverpool and signed on the "Wanderer" as an apprentice to make
his first deep sea voyage. In the Irish Sea the vessel was battered by heavy weather,
and was partially dismasted off the Tuskar Rock, a skysail yard fell and killed the
Captain. The Mate Shearer, took the vessel back to Liverpool, after spending 3 ½
days in Kingston affecting temporary repairs.

With Captain J. Brander in command the vessel sailed to San Francisco, then
back to Liverpool with grain. The next voyage was to Philadelphia, Calcutta and

Dundee. Under Captain Brander and then Captain T.S. Tupman the vessel voyaged to Calcutta, Barrow, Dundee, Philadelphia, Tacoma, Hiogo, Dunkirk, New York, Shanghai and Bristol. Whilst discharging at Bristol, Captain Tupman left and was replaced by Captain Bailey. The "Wanderer" left Bristol on April 13th 1901, in ballast and arrived in New York on July 9th here Bailey left and was replaced by Captain Dunning who loaded 119,207 cases of oil for Shangai. On January 3rd 1902, the "Wanderer" left Shangai in ballast and sailed to Tacoma to load grain. The vessel left Tacoma on February 11th and arrived in Cardiff, via Queenstown, on July 17th 1902.

The "Wanderer" left Cardiff on August 25th 1902, and most unusually she was in ballast and arrived at Philadelphia on September 21st. Captain Dunning loaded 120,000 cases of oil, sailed, and arrived at Kobe on March 8th 1903. From Kobe the vessel sailed in ballast to Tacoma and loaded wheat arriving off Queentown on 1st November and docked at Cardiff two days later. At 2.37 PM on 8th December, 1903, while shifting berths in Cardiff Docks, during violent weather, the "Wanderer" took charge of her tug and collided with the steamer "Strathmore", both vessels lost tops of their masts.

On December12th 1903, the "Wanderer" left Cardiff again, most unusually in ballast and was towed to Antwerp and loaded a general cargo for San Francisco. The vessel arrived at San Francisco on April 4th 1904. After unloading the vessel went to Port Blakely and loaded timber, leaving the timber port on February 14th 1905, and docked at Liverpool on July14th 1905. Only a part of the cargo was discharged and the vessel was towed to Cardiff to complete her discharge, arriving on 16th August 1905. After discharge she was dry-docked.

With Captain Thomas Dunning still in command the "Wanderer" left Cardiff on 24th September 1905, and was towed to Antwerp by the tug "Conqueror". General cargo was loaded for San Francisco and she sailed from Antwerp, November 15th 1905 and arrived at San Francisco on April 22nd 1906. Loaded with a mixed cargo of grain, honey and tinned fruits the vessel left on September 28th 1906, and docked at Liverpool, March 1st 1907.

After unloading the "Wanderer" left Liverpool on April 7th 1907, with slag ballast, towed by the tug "Sarah Jolene". Captain Dunning was accompanied by his wife. The tug towed the "Wanderer" to the mouth of the Elbe and after the "Wanderer" anchored in the Altenbruch Road the tug cast off. The "Wanderer" was to be towed to Hamburg the next day by the German tug "Lune", to load coke for Santa Rosalia. In the night the German steamer "Gertrud Woermann, of the Woermann Line, struck the "Wanderer" on the portside. All hands took to the boats and the vessel sank.

John Masefield wrote a poem about the sinking entitled "The Ending" and it contains these lines: "Then crash on the fenceless port broadside the Gertrud's steel bows struck, cutting deep, reeling back, grinding in again deeper, And over the Wanderer rolled at the force of the blow."

"Wanderer" (R. Hogben collection)

WILLIAM

A Severn trow built at the Bower Yard, Iron Bridge, Shropshire in 1809, she was an 'up-river' trow with an open hold and a single mast setting a square sail, and as such traded on the Severn - Gloucester, Tewkesbury etc until 1887. In 1887 the "William" was brought to the Saul boatyard, cut in half to be lengthened by 9 feet and rigged as a ketch, given a main mast with gaff mainsail and top-sail, a mizzen and bowsprit. The vessel was then used for trade in the Bristol Channel and regularly used the Ely Tidal Harbour.

By 1939, a hundred and thirty years old, the vessel was owned by Alfred Smith and Sons, of Bristol, and was used mainly on the coal run, Cardiff or Newport to Bristol with bunkering coal especially for Campbell's pleasure paddle steamers. Smith owned a number of trows including the "Alma", "Superb" and the "Spry", which has been fully restored and can be seen at Ironbridge.

On June 3rd 1939, the "William" loaded coal at Cardiff Bay for Bristol; she took a tow from one of Smith's steam coasters, the "Elemore". A very choppy sea was running and in the King Road, off the River Avon, the "William" was 'pooped' a sudden squall put a heavy sea over the vessel's stern and it flooded the open hold. The taking on of water and the strong wind capsized the trow. The Master, Captain George Warren, the Mate, Fred Walls, both drowned, but a crewman named Blower was rescued.

"William", a Severn trow being towed by the old steam coaster "Iron Duke",
entering Cardiff Docks in 1936 with what appears to be a 'mud-hopper' in the
background (W.I.M.M.)

WINDERMERE

The "Windermere was a three-mast square top-sail wooden schooner built at
Connah's Quay in 1890 by Ferguson and Baird (see "Katherine and May"), she was
of 174 tons with dimensions of 104.2 x 24.3 x 11.3. under her first master, Captain
"Jonty" Bennett, she was in the brick and tile trade from Connah's Quay mainly to
Belfast and other Irish ports. The vessel was owned by the Renay family who with
the Coppack family were the two principle ship-owning families at Connah's Quay.
The Renay's formed the Dee Ship owner's Mutual Insurance Association in 1880,
and in 1883 in partnership with the Coppack's bought the tug "Taliesin", that had
been built in Cardiff and brought the tug up to the Dee.

In September 1912 the "Windermere" was bought by Kearon and Tyrrell's and
they worked her in the Irish sea trades, especially coal from the Mersey ports and
the Cardiff Bay ports with timber or pit props on return. An engine was eventually
installed in 1927 and her topsail yards were removed. On September 18th 1931, the
vessel collided with a steam trawler the "Father O'Flynn" in the River Liffey and on
October 3rd 1945, in dense fog ran aground at Carnsore Point, Wexford, whilst
taking coal to Dungarvan.

The "Windermere" was a regular visitor to South Wales ports, including the Bay ports. On April 4th 1956, at 3 PM she left Barry in ballast for the short passage to Swansea and struck the Tusker Rock off Porthcawl, not to be confused with the Tuskar Rock in the Irish Sea. Fortunately the vessel grounded on a relatively flat shelf, even so the Mumbles lifeboat "William Gammon" stood by, as did an Air Sea Rescue launch from the RAF base at Porthcawl. On the next high tide the schooner was floated off and motored to Swansea and after an inspection returned to her home port of Arklow and was laid up.

In October 1956 the vessel was bought by French owners who placed her under the Costa Rican flag and brought her to Cardiff where she stayed until July 1957 when she left for the Mediterranean. During 1958 the vessel was abandoned in the Gulf of Lyons, the crew landing at Genoa.

"Windermere" at Whitehaven, Cumbria *c.* 1950's (T. Morgan collection)

"Windermere" fore-mast shewing roller-reefing gear etc., Whitehaven *c.*1950's
(T. Morgan collection)

YARRA

The "Yarra" was a sloop rigged Severn trow built at Bristol in 1880, the trow with various rigs was the 'local craft' of the river and its estuary and was to the Severn what the Thames barge was to the Thames and its estuary. The "Yarra" was a strongly built, wooden, flush deck trow of Net Reg. 56 tons, and was initially owned by the Cardiff ship-owner Daniel Gower who used her between the Bay ports and other Severn estuary ports. Around 1917 Gower sold the vessel to Alexander Watkins of Saul, who was an ex-trow skipper, who re-rigged the "Yarra" as a ketch and ran her in the Irish trade. Watkins eventually installed an engine and in 1949 the "Yarra" was de-rigged and became a motorised barge and later a towed barge, and in both guises was a familiar visitor to the Cardiff Bay ports.

Daniel Gower had a penchant for trows and owned at least eight, all loading coal at the Bay ports. The "Alice", built at Chepstow by George Fryers in 1868, at Fryer's Gunstock Wharf just downstream from the road bridge. Gower bought the vessel in 1899 and she was lost off the French coast in 1917, obviously taking advantage of the high wartime freights. Other trows included the "Brothers" built in 1841 at Brimscombe, the "Norah" built at Bridgwater in 1868 and sold by Gower to captain Leonard Smart (see "Jane") in 1932 for use as a houseboat at Uphill Wharf, the "Lovely Susan" built in 1839 at Whitminster, "Queen" built at Gloucester in 1854, "Squirrel" built in 1882 at Bridgwater, the "Theodore" built at Saul in 1871 and the "Yarra".

ZEBRINA

This vessel was built on the East Coast of England by H.H. Gawn of Whitstable in 1873 as a barquentine of 185 tons gross on dimensions of 109.1 x 23.9 x 9.9. After launching, the vessel was sailed out to the River Plate and was used to load in the shallow upper river reaches and then sail down river to transfer her cargo into the large oceanic sailing vessels anchored at the river's mouth. After about eight years the vessel returned to Britain and worked around the coasts, re-rigged as a double topsail schooner.

The vessel eventually came to trade in the Bristol Channel where her barge hull,

"Zebrina" (R. Hogben collection)

with a flatish bottom, and the fact that she did not need ballast made her ideal for the drying ports and harbours of the channel.

During the First World War the "Zebrina" loaded coal at Cardiff for St. Brieuc, in France, and the vessel was later found ashore just south of Cherbourg. She was in excellent order, all her gear and effects were intact but there was no sign of the master or crew. The weather was good and the incident became another of the numerous unsolved mysteries of the sea.

The vessel was saved, an engine was installed and she was rigged down to a fore and aft schooner, losing her topsail yards. After trading around the coasts she was converted into a motor vessel, caught fire and was hulked in the Solent and slowly fell apart.

GLOSSARY

ATHWART   Across the width of the vessel, at right angle to the fore-and-aft line.

BALLAST   Any heavy material such as iron or usually stone placed in the lower part of a sailing vessel to increase stability by lowering the centre of gravity. Some vessels were built with water ballast tanks.

BARQUE   A vessel of 3 or more masts, square-rigged on all but the rearmost mast, which is fore-and-aft rigged.

BARQUENTINE   A vessel of 3 or more masts square-rigged on the foremast only, fore-and-aft rigged on the others.

BRIG   A vessel with 2 masts both square-rigged.

BRIGANTINE   A 2 masted vessel square-rigged on the foremast only.

CRIMP   A man who procured crews for sailing vessels, usually by brutal and nefarious methods.

CUTTER   A single-mast vessel with 2 or more sails before the mast.

FORE-AND-AFT   Sails set along the vessels length rather than athwart.

FORECASTLE   On a vessel the forward part of the interior. Pronounced FO'C'S'LE.

FULL RIGGED SHIP   A vessel of 3 or 4 masts with square sails on all masts. One 5 mast ship was built the behemoth 'PREUSSEN', which set 59,000 square feet of sail.

GROSS TONNAGE   Measurement of the cubic capacity of a vessel's closed spaces, including the holds and deck house.

HOBBLERS   Men who assisted inward and outward bound sailing vessels, also hovellers and hufflers.

KETCH   A 2 masted vessel rigged fore-and-aft with the foremast the taller and the mizzen, rearmast, placed forward of the rudderpost.

MOONRAKER   A small square-sail set above the sky-sail.

SCHOONER   A fore-and-aft rigged vessel of two or more masts, the second mast carrying the main sail, some carried one or more square topsails on the foremast. The largest schooner was the mighty 'THOMAS W. LAWSON', with seven masts built at QUINCY, MASS in 1902 to carry 9,000 tons of coal.

SKY SAIL   A sail set above the royals on a square-rigged vessel.

SQUARESAIL   A four-sided sail hung from a spar called a yard.

TALL SHIP   Any full-rigged ship with sails above the royals, skysails, moonrakers etc.

TROW   From the Anglo-Saxon 'TROG' which soon appeared as 'TROUGH', applied to any hollowed out vessel. The Trow was originally an open single mast vessel setting one square-sail, to be seen on the river Severn. In the 19th century the vessels increased in size, became decked and Ketch rigged.

WIND JAMMER   A sailing vessel, usually a large one.

YARD   A spar from which a square-sail is hung.

YARD-ARM   The end of a yard.

BIBLIOGRAPHY

N. Ackland, *Schooner Captain,* Bradford Barton, 1972.

G. Aubry, *The Sea Dreamer,* 1957.

M. Bouquet, *No Gallant Ship,* Hollis and Carter, 1959.

M. Bouquet, *Westcountry Sail,* David and Charles, 1971.

J. Conrad, *A Personal Record,* English Review, Dec. 1908 - June 1909.

J. Conrad, *The Secret Sharer,* Harper's Magazine, Aug. - Sep. 1910.

H. Conway-Jones, *Gloucester Docks,* Alan Sutton, 1984.

G. Farr, *Somerset Harbours,* Christopher Johnson, 1954.

G. Farr, *Ships and Harbours of Exmoor,* Exmoor Press, 1970.

C. Green, *Severn Traders,* Black Dwarf Publications, 1999.

Dr. B. Greenhill, *The Merchant Schooners* VOL I, II, David and Charles, 1968.

Dr. B. Greenhill and Ann Gipfard, *The Merchant Sailing Ship,* David and Charles, 1970.

Dr. B. Greenhill and John Hackman, *Herzogin Cecilie,* Conway Maritime Press, 1991.

Dr. B. Greebhill and John Hackman, *The Grain Races,* Conway Maritime Press, 1986.

Dr. B. Greenhill, *The Ship. The life and death of the Merchant Sailing Ship,* National Maritime Museum, 1980.

Captain M.J. Henderson, *Farewell Pamir,* Author N.Z. 1990's.

A.A. Hurst, *Square-riggers. The Final Epoch 1921-1958,* Teredo Books, 1972.

A.A. Hurst, *Medley of Mast and Sail* VOL I AND VOL II, Teredo Books, 1976 and 1981.

G. Kahre (Ed. B.Greenhill), *The Last Tall Ships,* Conway Maritime Press, 1978.

B. Lubbock, *The Log of the Cutty Sark,* Brown, Son and Ferguson, 1949.

B. Lubbock, *The Last Windjammers* VOL I AND VOL II, Brown, Son and Ferguson, 1949.

B. Lubbock, *The Nitrate Clippers,* Brown, Son and Ferguson, 1932.

Dr. L. Morrish, *Goodnight Irene,* February Press, 1985.

G. Mote, *The Westcountrymen. Ketches and Trows,* Badger Books, 1986.

W.H.(Ben) Norman, *Tales of Watchet Harbour,* Author, 1988.

R. Simper, *British Sail,* David and Charles, 1972.

R. Simper, *Britain's Maritime History,* David and Charles, 1982.

W.J. Slade (Ed. B.Greenhill), *Out of Appledore,* Conway Maritime Press, 1959.

W.J. Slade and B. Greenhill, *Westcountry Ketches,* Conway Maritime Press, 1974.

M.K. Stammers, *West Coast Shipping,* Shire Publications, 1976.

Prof. H. Thesleff, *Farewell Wind jammer,* Thames and Hudson, 1951.